MUSCULAR
POETRY

Muscular
Poetry

By Kemo Chen

MUSCULAR POETRY

iUniverse books may be ordered through booksellers or by contacting:

iUniverse
1663 Liberty Drive
Bloomington, IN 47403
www.iuniverse.com
1-800-Authors (1-800-288-4677)

ISBN: 978-1-5320-7085-3 (sc)
ISBN: 978-1-5320-7086-0 (e)

Print information available on the last page.

iUniverse rev. date: 03/11/2019

MUSCULAR POETRY

There are all types of poetry, some about flowers and bees, and some of unrequited love and passions.

This is not a collection of thoughts like that, but instead a gathering of notions that define in some way what it is like to be a man. A man who sees the world in different shades of light gray and white, and sometimes black; and at other times, with the darkness that comes from deep within that allows light to enter sparingly.

We all have influences, and mine are of strong men, who have lived otherwise ordinary lives, but found some hope inside of themselves, and expressed it through long form, poetry and prose. In the end, each a story teller, prepared to narrate their lives and, by doing so, inform us all of life's meaning.

Words were both sword and shield.

No judging of other poets and styles that captured the same themes in different images. Instead, a robust presentation of existence, from the streets, the bars, and the living rooms of our modern age.

No holds barred, the rough and tumble exposed, fears and hopes in a constant battle for dominance.

All these experiences found their way to the page.

Bukowski, Fante, Lewis, Elliott, and another basket of great men who found their way to poetry. Some writing on shopping bags and old paper. Others in tiny apartments, by candles, or in foxholes. These are the thoughts of men troubled by their own travails, hopes and desires.

And mine as well, unresolved issues, of all men after the holy grail:

happiness and peace of mind.

KC 2019

EXPIRATION DATES

Everything organic has one
Eggs, that loaf of bread in the plastic bag, even your Bud
A time certain, when it is over and done

To be discarded, tossed, or buried
Before
It decays, stinks, when what was nutritious
Is just so much garbage

Products have them, men do not
Although easier it might be to know
When it all would end, by looking for a label
A barcode on your wrist

Gershwin did not know, while writing famous tunes
That the smell of burning rubber was a tumor
Grapefruit size in his brain, that July 11th, in 1937
Would be his expiration date

Racing his green Mustang over hilly roads
Steve McQueen could not imagine that
A few years hence, he would be laying on a table in
Mexico
Taking coffee enemas and drinking God knows what

To cure him from mesothelioma, from ripping out
asbestos, as a young Marine
Expiration date: November 7, 1980

Heart throb, Luke Perry, a later day James Dean
Has a massive stroke at 52.
A star of some proportion, known for a zip code show
90210
Expiration date : March 4, 2019

And General Ulysses S Grant had no time to ponder
Through every battle, skirmish, and war, when limbs and
guts rested at his boots
That all those cigars, and campfire food would turn a
scratchy throat into
A life sapping cancer
Pain became his companion, even as poverty loomed,
writing his grand memoirs through it,
As Mark Twain, got him a cash advance, to help soothe
the old soldiers worries
But, by July 23, 1885, it all ended, on that expiration date

Even the most mighty fall to it, eventually
Alexander the Great drank himself into a fever, after two
nights
Being drop dead, blazing, drunk.
In Babylon, Nebuchadnezzar II's palace

His came 11 June 323 B.C. He conquered most of the known world until
His expiration date

For the rest of us?
If you knew the date, would you change any of this life you
Are creating for yourself?

Believe in predestination
A God given path
Some great book of life, with your date in it
Unrevealed
Or is it just all crap and chaos
Live the life you can
Find the path that gives you some meaning, purpose, some heart
Or just gets you out of bed

Maybe before you are consumed and discarded like a banana peel
You might just get some happiness out of it all.

THE RESERVOIR

There is a vast, empty reservoir of cynicism somewhere in
our brain
deeper in some empty at birth filled by unloved
disappointment
ambition, lost, loss, broken promises.
Some dreams, disease, a shallowness,
petty miseries, is filled by life seen one way as; chaotic,
overwhelmed by the outside marked by other plans, not
ours.

And it fills over time and overflows and overflows
into a river of sarcasm, anger, and mostly frozen lakes of
inaction.

Drain.. Drain the reservoir of cynicism.
You don't need it anymore, it will drown you and
everything you wanted,
will be consumed by it.

THE THREE GREAT REVOLUTIONS

Everyone thinks of revolutions of politics, of blood and guts, of guillotines,
barricades rushed by men
and men destroyed by one ideology overtaking another.

None of them really changed much.
Some did for a moment.
The natural end of tyranny, divine right, plutocracy, the ruling elites,
all fell in, some rose again. And history moved forward, or so. Some thought.

The first revolution came from the desert and the old man of the ancient book.
For Abraham heard from God, and was touched by him to believe in him. A simple message to be heard.
A message uttered from son to son, that there was just one creator. All the idols, the statues gold and not, could not bring what was created to the created.
Jehovah was one God. A real revolution.

Thousands of years pass.
Who does not the Mary and John tale. Jesus arrives.

A revolution more powerful than any, that starts with a
birth, a crucifixion ends it, for the Romans.
Then defied by a resurrection.

One message on another. There is one God, I am his son,
whoever believes in me shall have everlasting life. And,
treat all men as you want to be treated. Those are the rules
you need to follow and the only rules you need to know.
And then the Enlightenment came, Locke and Rousseau,
Paine, and Jefferson, with their social contracts, and a
simple belief that all men are created equal and endowed
by Abraham's creator with certain rights, unalienable.
They said.

This third revolution seems somehow tenuous.
Where the people created a government to serve them and
not a state to rule them. And it has not been 300 years,
yet, to see and judge it yet.
How resilient
To have worked, from Abraham through the Kings
of Israel, the Romans and Visigoths, the Babylonians
and Assyrians, dictators and demagogues, Nazis and
Communists, and to have survived it all.
If this fails,
Will there be another, must there be
to preserve God's work.

ADDITIONS

More men more men settle early on everything.
What they will work for and at who they will love
bed and discard
some eat the same crap until their arteries explode.

Walk the same stairs drive the same road make
love the identical way to all their women.

I remain with the limited vocabulary of a modern
man, grunting and nodding their way to the
nursing home.

Change never comes
pattern overcomes variety, variety dies in a rut of a
life of subtractions.

A few are adders plus siders,
they add women try all the, Sutra stuff. Screw
their friends wives once,
spend a night with a transsexual, mountain bike
Mongolia

Climb the Matterhorn
talk to their children and even go to dinner with
an ex-wife.
Learn Mandarin,Tai Chi, and practice Bushido.
Cook omelettes for their daughters
cry for their dead children and stand for a cause of
the moment, constantly.

Choose the additional life,
fill the rut with activity, and never ever wonder
what the other life is like.

Better to have no one to bury you,
than have a funeral down the block from the
bar you sat at every Monday night for the last 45
years.

OF ALL THE BEDS

of all the beds in West L.A.,

yours was the one that took me on journeys to
faraway exotic places I've never been

Warm waters, sarong places, with birds of paradise
and soft breezes running through your hair.

Hair that always smelled fresh even in those
cigarette days.

Soft wolfing eyes, suggesting an essential animal
under cold crisp sheets.

Beds blue, pine wood, four posted, beneath puffy
comforters.

Always a holy place, where all the world's weight
lifted,
and an ancient coupling transported to young
souls to a simple altered state.

Where your cheek on my shoulder, met signaling to the universe, leave us alone, we are at peace here.

Every night I dream of it, my place on that bed.

Once yours then ours, now yours again.

Unachievable, place of solace gone,

Lost in the dark night of a shattered love.

OH WHAT I LIKE

She wants to know this, pants suited shrink, who
knows some Freud a bit of Jung, mostly Erickson,
Dwyer, and Oprah.

What I like, oh,
the feeling of walking onto a running track, never
knowing if that's the day you run with wind and
no effort returning to 18, on another magic oval,
full of possibility,
and I like
the finish line of anything and sweat, mine
and that flush moment, engorged, moments,
when she rests her head on your shoulder naked,
wordless, without motion, loves static electricity.
Sizzling, and you pray that the world will STOP.
Suspended.

And then I like

Listening to a backyard rose grow, sitting alone in the
sun, surrounded by blades of wet grass, covered in dew
with a squirrel leaping from roof to ground, and the way,
a sentence sounds pure and solely crafted, uncollaborated.

And I like this woman in the other chair,
who likes everything but me and I'd like to stop
searching for a lost path. The one with abandoned
dreams. The one without sunlight, that is under a
jungle canopy

AT THE A AND W

There are fewer of them, where we used to drive in
to get out mug of root beer and everyone still ate
burgers.

A stop in unlikely places to rest, crap,
and find something you could miss elsewhere
between a Tyrannosaurus of concrete and a stucco
Triceratops

Down by the casino. The Marengo Indians built
next to this outlet mall populated by Asians
bused in from God knows where, surrounded by
extended Hispanic families with classic faces from
a Kahlo painting frame by wide smiles.

All of them shopping for pillows, sandals, running
through Gucci and Prada eating sweet kettle corn
leaving trails of kernels on parking lots, wind
swept clean.

I sit in ½ booth facing the sun as it loped behind
snowcapped mountains, San Jacinto next.

And I want nothing epistemological. Either. Just
someone to care enough here. To give me the
Heimlich in case I choke on the cuisine

I inhale a fine fish sandwich. Listen to a table
of college kids all Asian talk about football,
cosmetics, nothing deeper. A day after Christmas.

It is 35 out there along the I 10. I do not want to
move, hoping destiny will walk in at number 145
to my 144.
And I will hit kismet in this half booth.

As the sun dissolves the college kids depart,
clean their table, number 145 is a family of four.
Looking to buy a trunk full of Nikes.

At least the mug was frosted, and the root beer
tasted exactly the same as it did when I was a
teenager with a hot car, a few girls who would
have sex with me,

And possibilities, plenty of them.

A COLD NIGHT IN HOBOKEN

down the streets were Sinatra sang, past Johnny's
saloon.
After that last round, he fell over on his side.
His soft body shielding the soul of grit and gristle.
This man who knew how the world actually
worked knowing always
who lied, died, told truth and all those who failed
each day to accomplish whatever it was they
thought they needed to do.

He knew them all. Smoked, too much drink with
them all.
He mostly spoke to them through a dialogue of
paper, and electrons, while chomping cigars and
popping nicotine tablets.
He consumed everything until everything
consumed him.

Organ by organ, until tubes replaced cigars,
oxygen tanks replaced Jim Beam, the streets
he so loved, gone silent
before the news man's dawn, kicked another cycle
of story after story forward to another deadline.
One night a deadline he could not see nor meet.

Alone. As the wind blew the snow, and the streets were barely plowed, as they always were, on this last bitter night. Finally, silenced, Damon Runyon's last iconoclastic man,

Hoboken fell silent, and Red Hook wept.
The last newsman, of the old school, is dead, rolled off his bed sober, unlike O'Neill.
Eulogies ahead, will never capture him.

EVERYONE GETS LAID
AT FUNERALS

Less so at weddings
Something to do with a fear of being lost,
forgotten, or just being alone.
A bond of sorrow, or recognition that the fates
passed you by
The wind knifes through you as you walk the
blocks from garage to funeral parlor
No one is glad to arrive

When everyone follows in overheated cars and
limos to the widows home
The mood lifts

Her hands are warm.
This ex-wife now considering this once famous
man who she could not control live with or
dismiss.
Hair colored sandy, hazel eyes that have seen him
laugh and cry, rarely, but mostly stare out over
the pool as dusk came to a backyard in Connecticut.

A once 20 game winner, with all his hair, and arm
that could still win 30 games, roams the
sunroom hugging a sea of women dressed in black.

The men gather outside, with enormous cigars,
clouds of blue /grey smoke
   telling stories, as they do, when one of their own
      slips from comrade and friend to corpse.

It does not matter what the cause, or calamity that
fell him. Cocaine or booze.
Only that he is gone and has left them to their
insanity.

The tears fade, the whiskey flows.

No one wants to go home. The cars are turned
over, they run without pilots until they are warm
enough to enter. Manhattan is far away, hotel
rooms closer.

Everyone is lonely. Funerals do that.

The lost find others who are lost. Some find their
way to the same bed to forget what is, and have

something with another for a few hours before
they must return to what it is that defines them or
is at least their life.
And the widow weeps, and cannot sleep

MADNESS

Comes from small things going wrong, not the distant
black holes, unexplainable politicians, or where to store
our radioactive waste

Madness arises as the egg breaks
in your hand dribbles on your knee,
the coffee burns your tongue at its tip,
you sliced through a tomato into your index finger and
blood, egg, and coffee
drown you.

Thoughts of a triumphant day come and go. And you sigh
that the good forces are in some other place, coaxing a tall
brunette into bed, hitting 21 at Caesars, having a clean
colonoscopy, even then

Madness arises.
When your knees are so shot. You can't run or play
basketball for months,
you've missed sex for eight months,
have lost your muse, no Penthouse or Playboy can save
you. You are being chased by banshees
And have nothing left, about to surrender

And you haven't smiled this year and it's August

Every day you resolve to overcome all of it.

Predetermined fates have chained you to the rock of
Prometheus.
And you decide to break free of the chains and leave
before Zeus' Eagle removes your liver at dawn, only to
have it regrow and be removed again at dusk.

But without the madness.
What would life be. You know you were never happy with
serenity, smiles, and good spirits, anyway.

Stay mad. The world doesn't care. And neither should you.

DEAL

There is a craft to it

looking for gold, talking through, endlessly the
scheme,the deal
hear it coming across pastrami, and blow across herbal tea
caught between bites of some chopped grass and endive.

Between gulps of ever so perfect bubbles in Italian water
bottles, the deal bubbles, rises and is burped up.

Shut up, turn off the Benz.
The valets the waitresses, busboys, hear it rumbling like
gas and an old man's colon, these deals for movies, cars,
stars and
nothing leading to nowhere deals

To keep people going, hoping that between bites and pills.
Maybe
just one deal is consummated,
joined without bull shit to let something result, now lost
in discussion and behind the liars veil, put the fork down
sign something

One deal, in this life, just one.
And a lifetime supply of TUMS

ONE LEG

Some are for breasts, tit or ass, the perverse nape of her
neck, foot, or face

Captured by it all. I sat with the model type, 5 foot eight,
stunning structure on a face that has seen Milan, Paris
and New York
The usual parts and signage.
In a minidress exposing thigh and suggesting an inviting
crotch.
Not unusual at all until she walks to the podium to talk
about cancer, and I watched her hobble a bit.

Bone cancer came and took her leg.

The runway that was her career gone. Described it in
enough detail to bring tears to every table as she described
the surgery, then the recovery, and her determination to
return to the life she knew.
Everyone stood.
She came back with a plaque, to thunderous applause.
Not bad for a night in New Jersey by exit 14.

The story was too much to absorb
she seemed to know that she had a more powerful allure
than before.
Discretion and poise were not removed by a surgeon's
knife.
She disrobed as if she were an Egyptian queen. And placed
the leg on a green towel as she eased her body backward
onto the bed.

And with that
Nothing else remarkable, just the old in and out, but
with a sweetness that came from a perfumed mist that
moleculed the air.

With every breath along the amorous journey,
you wanted to cry for her,
but you stayed strong,
afraid that she would find you weaker than she,
so you pursued each other quietly.

In the greatest hope
that you could coax a smile out of a face
that had had its own lifetime of pain.

AFM

sometimes you just know you're not going to get where
you're going.
Been to the Santa Monica hotel, fancy now, overlooking
the beach for every type of horseshit meeting imagined
American Film Market,
Just sanctified the process of getting cash for a film
Especially if that's someplace filled with 5'3" women all
dressed in black and 5 foot, 7 inch men and tight, narrow
shouldered, Armani's blazers.

Lumpy folks, with cash,
all looking to buy, sell, acquire some poor guy's film or
some rich fucks distorted vision of what people want.
Horror, soft porn, and a few, very few westerns
so I drive to the beach thinking I'll take in a seminar for
30 bucks. I don't have just to meet a guy with a Z name
like Zorro or Zuni, who sits on a fund for movies if you
make it in New Mexico.

But the sun is out, the marine layer is leaving
warm enough
to run shirtless

warm enough to watch the young guy nuzzle his nose up
his girlfriends crack laying on a blanket in her thong, and
its California, everyone is so self involved no one cares

Who needs the money for some project made just to grab
some Z man's Dough. I do,
but not enough to trade the beach for a seminar in a hotel
room by the sea, filled with people in black begging for
green.

ANN, THANKS

at 16, in the 60's, the only nude women you see are in
glossy photographs in pages of expensive magazines which
names that belie their purpose.

Gallery
Genesis
High Society or even Esquire
with Angie Dickinson's bare butt out for full view and
occasionally
you see and touch another 16 or 18-year-old as horny as
you are, and she is your gateway to adolescent nirvana
So for a guy to see a full-bodied large tit and full ass
woman, not many choices
There was burlesque. But you couldn't get in until one old
dame
Anne Curio, put the girls on tour there in Valley Forge of
all places.
One cannon shot away from a bad winter for Washington
and his boys.
That review turned 16-year-olds into hard men with
new dreams of colossal women with tassels on their tits,
revolving in circles.
G strings
enormous ass

red lips and
joy.

They toured the country,
opened the door of carnal desire, a door that never closed,
always hoping to find one of them in your life. A boy's
dream over 40 years.
A sense memory of a statuesque stripper, and troupe of
bawdy gals, gyrating
Lighting the young mans fire of desire

FROGS

it's all concrete, now
asphalt for 3000 cars,aisles of oranges, celery and frozen
everything stores
for a neighborhood of people who live in homes with
small lawns and big dreams.
Once it was a swampy field of mud holes and slender grass
that waved to us as boys looking for some adventure where
the streets gave way to what was left of Penn's Woods.
There was one portal where we collected pond scum and
one day a frog.

On that day we were Huck and Tom,
until a tall senior and a Father Judge jacket took the frog
and beat it dead with a rock.
Took my buddies frog put it in a paper sack and
jackbooted away its life.
Right there.
Hard lesson.
A brainless thug was the apex predator of the
neighborhood, and that day we were cowards and watched
and did not fight.
You carry the indignity and the cowardice
of the smallest events for a lifetime.

You can learn how to hate injustice,

the damage unchecked might, without conscience can do,

in the strangest places.

There is terror, when no one stands for justice.

When we were older

by two years, the field was concrete.

A Sears store on that place where the frogs died. We had

grown some .

Now we tracked him, that neighborhood Nazi, who so

frightened us

and we grabbed him and broke his right knee.

Even frogs deserve retribution

FROM BEHIND

Most guys like it this way.

On her hands and knees ready for an ancient right
propelling you to an apelike time before Homo erectus
becomes Homo sapiens.
When men stalked their women even as evolution had
given pendulous breasts
to attract men face-to-face.
But the butt remained the center ring of the sexual circus.
The breasts ruled in the face-to-face that only men and
women could do, unless you were a two toed sloth and no
one wanted that.

From breasts on it was their world, their dance, and the
chains came on.

Never been the same again.

Millions of years of evolution, equality, feminism, cultural
advancement.

So when you get a woman from behind. It's a throwback,
primeval in its way, not just another pose, but a distinct
step back in time.

And it seems as you thrust back and forth. You're the master, listening to no one
unrestricted.
Nowhere, no balls, busted, no deductions.

Just one damn attractive partner with a great ass and her canals' grip on you, a calamity of pleasure.

And you are directly wired to your ancient ancestors, who before mortgages, responsibility, and therapy, thought from behind was a great recreation.

Good luck explaining that to the woman below you.

PANAMA

Every bank had a guard with a long barreled 12 gauge
shotgun
Outside
Always with the same eyes, wide open, black and as big as
pancakes.

I ran on the streets at dawn alone.
No one near me,
an outcast in this part of the machine gunned stronghold
of the deposed Noriega
along the canal and slowly back.

Pretending to understand
acknowledging the difference between us, one guard
raised his shotgun, an over and under and cracked a smile,
I smelled of nervous sweat.

We came for fast money,
but we were scammed.
By the time we got back to the hotel we knew,
the money we hoped to raise was staying here and not
going home with us.

Two hapless desperados on foreign turf afraid now for our
lives
, but soothed
by three German gals swimming, topless,
and in black thongs.
With a beefy boyfriend who rubs oil on their backsides.

Lovely Place, Panama.

LIMES

across from the 40-year-old roses and the scruffy backyard
filled with dog crap that no one picks up except on
Sundays
is a strong trunked Lime tree, that offers up large green
globs, without effort or trauma
a miracle of creation.

Branches weighted with clumps of five or six and efficient
colorful fruit bounty.
Bringing them into a kitchen bowl,
thinking they would bring color and ingredients for some
guacamole or lime colored pie.
But away from yard and stem
they shrivel unused,
reduced in size and changing color and texture.

All fruits carrying seeds,
even mine, untouched,
forgotten
Without water, a place to grow, or enough sun to warm.
They shrink and shrivel
lost and wasted in a bowl untouched.

Tomorrow I will throw them away.
There are two symbolic, these fruits once grown,
untouched and unused
that shrivel grow smaller in turn color.

These limes are the Dorian Gray for my balls.

MO'S

There I was there I was counting my way up the road to
Diamondhead. I glanced at a dark haired woman.
Breasts sucked up by a joggers bra,
dark eyes, cleavage, tight ass on an old road bike.
Watching me attempt to get to the turnaround before her

So I stopped anyway to watch erect surfers riding along
waves, and then she said hello, saying she thought of
hitching a ride on me up the hill.

So I small talk her
ineptly
Taking a snapshot of her face and thought what her bleach
mustache revealed on the hair on the rest of her
so I'm pulsating in the humidity
but missed the opportunity, as always
to get to know her for a drink
dinner, and really embark on an explorers journey

After a while these MO's add up.
The same modus operandi day after day.
No change
life that might have had adventure, stuck in a gully with
unclimbable sides.

Everything becomes a muse, a daydream,
a lost opportunity to explore someone else, who might
actually want to explore you.

So devoted you are to 1 foot before another,
on an endless linear path to a turnaround and back again.
Too much memory, reverie, and inaction.

Regrets pile up, even in paradise.

QUIET NOW

There are men who are always talking
Never shut their face
So much do they admire what
Comes out of their mouths

From brain to vocal cords with no buffer
Or walls of thought
Aware of nothing more than themselves
Without pauses or inhaling breaths

Usually they believe, we all want to hear
Their views of politics, baseball, your wife, his children,
And, of course, how right he is about everything

When there were corner bars, the mouth,eventually sat
alone
And when he put together the wrong views in wrong
sentences
Uncle Tommy would put down his beer, walk over and
gently tell him to shut up

When he did not
We all smiled
Tommy hit him in the solar plexus

Because he hurt his hand once with a uppercut
And the beer vomit, was more pleasing than all the
opinions

The Buddha knew and advised
To speak when
It will have meaning, help, correct an error
Soothe another, warm a soul

If it is not necessary
Be quiet
When it is
Be kind
And let the other guy get a word in from time to time

EGGS AND TOAST

When you get up after sex
With someone you barely know
It is always awkward
Whether to stay
Whether to go

There is always conversation
Avoiding how it went
Afraid to review it at all
Talk of the weather, the job, her girlfriends,
Whether you will go to work
Grab the subway or a cab across town
You can share

It is always good for you
All that you could do
To run through every position and enter every spot
Where bodies can enter and join in
Ecstasy, or as close as you can get

Sharing in and outs
As close as you can get
So uncomfortable still to speak

Except to offer thanks
Like a boy to his mother

Then she breaks four eggs and flips them, in a black
old pan
Puts wheat bread into a toaster
Pours orange juice
And you both sit down
And pretend that you are, at least, friends,
After a night of being lovers

And a calm overcomes you
As she smiles

CHUCK

In a bright orange Gull Winged Lamborghini. He would park on sidewalks
wave to proper Boston secretaries
and gate crash.
Anything.
At lunch we drive to a rusting strip bar in Revere. He had dark eyes in the skull with the face of Cassius, and he would mesmerize the dancers.
One by one, they'd crawl to him turn their asses to his nose.
He was both magnet and benefactor.

With each bite of his roast beef. Another story was exposed.
Soldiering. Vietnam.
Assassin.

Then he wrapped his arm around me chokehold style
squeeze until I grabbed his balls to get free
Then he talk about the next caper like Sinatra in Ocean's Eleven. Years passed,
and there he was in a bomber jacket,
in a joint in Washington DC.

Prosperous now, he folded 20s into their G strings. Two
dancers squatted, pulled back their G strings
snatched the bills into oblivion.
He spoke of un-piloted drones far before their time,
he saw battles with radical Islam
before anyone knew they were there,
and he longed for another mission that would take him
there.
He was a man of dark rooms and loud music, and I look
for him there in those places.
Liar or madman, some of both.

Flamboyant men and pirates
have given way to quiet men who have been, domesticated,
frightened by life and who have lost their stones.
He does not roll a boulder up the hill and smile at the
insanity of it.

Every hill has its own adventure.
Every turn a path to another story.
At one moment in the dark, strip joint,
The next in a hut in some godforsaken place with a Glock
in his hand, inhaling the rare air that only comes to men
who are never in the same place twice.

I GIVE UP

I give up you win.

Whatever contest this is

in life and attempts to hold it together are lost on me.

My buzzer is broken can't get anyone to notice,

Alex Trebek, my buzzer doesn't work. I am out of answers.

Category: contribution answer: do you have one left.

Wasted by this life almost ashamed to admit

it to anyone but myself.

Out of desire

doubled over in pain night and morning,

worn out by meetings without result,

paychecks that build no equity, addict, that will not rise

and has no reason to

Oh the friends say it is classic depression, but I fear that it

is not.

Instead, it is but a wasted life now seen as poorly regarded,

humorless, passion seeking, yet unfulfilled.

Shallow grave stuff.

What fire burned is smoke only after the water is tossed on a campfire.
That wet burned smell that covers the forest in the night or
a house after the fire .
Reeking of it, burned wood half ignited charred, without a single ember

All fires turn black,
leaving the orange flame only a memory in the desert starry night,
flame extinguished now gone of love and women and family.
Once connected, all off to other fires, as there is no warmth here.

No details left to tell. No new faces. No one left with fire still to burn inside them.
So it is gone here so it is gone here, Alex, is the final answer.

I've become a blackened pit on an abandoned beach?

BALANCED TIPPED

Is there some balance of life, I've missed.

It seems there is more sorrow and pain in most lives than
joy, not by a little, but by far.

A bar graph of sorrow three times as high as joyful things.

Most spend life waiting for the good of things.
Living the righteous life finding the odds wrong.
5-2 sorrow, big game this life.
In the households. The odds,
a six deck shoe of uncountable cards, and we all expect an
ace and face cards. and the odds are worse
than 5 to 2, but we wait and wait.

And there is suffering, death, illness,
loneliness, old man's pain, young men's wonders,
personal furies, having great sex and then any sex.
Some wait for un conditional love, from someone who is
not your mother.
Or a few moments of bliss when you want the planet to
stop, just stop, for that one thing you really love.

Maybe you get it once, twice or a few times a week,
but weigh that against the stone on your back all that
weight for so little time without it.
No contest here.

That's not to say there aren't those special folks who only
see joy
even when they're swimming through a lake of crap just
like the rest of us.
And they swim through it with a smile, I suppose.

There is a universe out there that is not out there,
but is within that I could re-create if I wanted to that
which set the balance straight,
where men are meant to be happy and balanced and full
of the wonder of it all.
No one else will reset it.
This unbalanced life.
I know I can decide to do it. The wonder is why I have
lived so long, not moved towards any of it.
Pretending to find peace, when a war is raging in my gut.

AS LONG AS THERE IS

A long black heavy bag. The world is safe for my anger,
unsettled lunacy, seething hate
unbridled depression.

Whack Whack it goes
hard left, right to the body,twisting from the hip
power up from the legs faster
Bop Bop

Sweat comes now imagined, the faces of one foe to
another.
This one is hurting her. That one is cheating me that one
is taxing me.
In the mirror, I am shuffling, in this old age with my
declining good looks
receding hairline.
Still, I hit it

Harder now without rest. 300 punches then 100 more. 50
jabs 250 power punches as it goes.
Whack Whack, Bop. Bop

Therapy without the jabber

They watch me, the old women. The tall black guys
after their court game and the small hippie girls at the
Stairmaster's

And they are worried that I'll die right here in front of
them and they wonder where does this old man's ferocity
come from,
under the red gloves. My hands turn raw, poorly wrapped,
no Dundee, no Freddie Roach

I know all this pounding will not change any of it
It is in some way a coward's way to inner peace. Hitting
this bag
not confronting the actual villains in my life
but I go on

With my insides intact because there is this bag this long
black heavy bag that has earned its PhD in my pain

I HAVE WALKED THE DARK ROADS

Winding unlit places where grief is.

Loneliness is a rest stop where the road kill lay

Untouched ideas, visions, un found gold
those trips never taken
smiles unseen
Up this Parkway on a cold March day. Under this cold
rain slipping on some canyon road,
searching for lost youth and a young man's dreams

A roadway by a beach alone,
Hoping the sun rise will force,
upon long closed eyes, squinting for a sign of deliverance,
walking the black road seeing darkness shadows in the
night of all those fears
that have kept me here.
I am not alone here. I hear the others shuffling, wanting a
beacon.
Fellow walkers, mostly deluded that this is the only place
for them.
These roads have taken me nowhere.
I know there is more to see,

even happiness,

but a few yards over there, where I must go or all will be lost.

This misery I so cherish is a lantern with no light.

Is it time to leave the dark road?

And walk into the light.

THE OLDEST JOURNEY

Odysseus had it right, away for 20 years on a ship with
some hearty men

Thinking he was on his way to something
discovering himself,
his weaknesses and passions.

Always thinking he would escape to the quiet life with
Penelope and
her wide ass and soft nipples,
on his secret bed entrapped by an ancient tree.
Sirens challenged him, but he survived.

Cyclops storms and his wife's hateful suitors,
Somehow he knew the gods would direct his ship through
tossed sea, away from danger.

Such faith is hard to come by now, even though our
modern journeys are hardly harsher

Give me a one eyed monster and island of sirens an easier
battle than
the IRS, wives, and just plain making ends meet.

And where and when do the gods release me home to my bed and to some Penelope.

My secret is the same. I have become the journey, I have been fooled, like Odysseus.

Who will release,me home.

God's, with a cosmic wish,
can you command me home, at last, away from this journey to a warm room and quiet bed.

LILACS AND JACARANDAS

I walk on concrete and asphalt, drifting, and in a trance,
forcing thoughts out and away exhaling into a morning
layer of ocean mist.

One attempt again to amble long enough without aim
or destination until a calm comes, if it can be noticed,
without form or starting point or middle course,
meandering.

Noticing nothing really at all until destiny reveals itself,
as likely as a lotto prize toward some finish line.

Only the lilacs overtake me
fragrance of some genetic cellular force like what I've
splashed on my newly shaved boys face, lilac, a memory of
an odor representing youth, prowess, capability and broad
reachable horizons.

I walk through a garden of lilacs and trees and lavender
that blooms spreading a purple carpet on block after
block.
Only the droppings of the neighbors dogs harm it,
crapping over all of it, blocking the lilac fragrances
inserting their own.

The crap and fecal fumes present the oppressive reality inserted like barbs of steel into my already damaged psyche, still I am walking through the lavender leaves dodging the crap, always dodging the crap, seeing the leaves, lavender, and inhaling an aroma that brings me back, to recall long walks that brought thoughts of triumph and possibility.

Inhaling and exhaling spring, and it's promise of beginnings

ALA MOANA

Weathered face, scars on shoulder and arm,
enough white hair to mark a kahuna's mane.
Sprinkled with tufts of white on an old chest, arm and
thigh.
Smooth face old man paddles kayak slowly from the reef
towards a quiet sheltered patch of blue/green ocean.

A sinking Hawaiian sun creates an orange backlight
he glides to shore only to jump into calmer waters and
swim 600 strokes.
Whatever came before is gone from his bones,
wounds, mistakes, losses.
All the journeys he chose others, others chose him
where he was taken to some place that was far from his
dreams.
Knowing that you can become,, defined by what you are
doing rather than what you want to do.

Too much running away and from, to this place.
Finally, to paddle and stroke.
Finding a new life.
Rhythm to this, learning, wondering
why it took so long to arrive here

And how the other life lost its purpose long ago,
chains self-imposed bound him there.
400 strokes now towards that far wall, the pain of all
those past days
today lost between breath and stroke.

Put me on that beach. Place me in that water. Float out to
that sunset.

Just one warm night
, one sunset orange,
all the cold damp thoughts, blank stares, and wrong
choices
forgotten
across a protected lagoon.

PRANAYAMA

Who moves so quickly now
That they are breathless
Unable to just inhale and exhale
And relax,with each natural action

Everyone it seems
Is searching for some way to
Slow it all down, so they can say
Anything of merit, turn down the pace
Some what to help find the way and not fall on their face

There are caves of monks in orange
Breathing in and out all day
In mountains of Shangri La
Covered in wet sheets
Emitting heat and steam from bodies powered by
devotion and
Focused breath

Women in yoga pants and tank tops in rooms across LA
Are practicing in and outs in
The 4-7-8 way

Hold a nostril and breath in for four
Hold for seven
Exhale for 8
Do it four times and get to twenty
And use this everyday, you need a break from
The pressures of the day

I know these women, work with them, and play
I wish they were as calm as the monks are still today
For all the inhale and exhales that offers escape
When engaged in 4-7-8
The search takes more
Sometimes being breathless is not such a bad thing
At all

MOVING ZAZEN

I have crossed my legs before candle and fire
sat at creeks slow running brooks before crashing foaming
ocean waves.

Stood on one leg crane like in gardens and yards on
human mornings dripped into fragrances of Hawaiian
flora.

Searching for a Zen trance, no tomorrow, no past
anything breath in and out a lifetime.

But thoughts come and I try to stop them, but they come
So I run, with no mind. On trail and blacktop, with semi
trucks and mothers and kids in SUV's
Everything slows
destinations dissolve with my sweat those worries, fears,
evils that chronic tight neck of my life.

I am moving I am alone, but not lost
faster, harder pace transports my spirit and finding it
think of nothing for an hour or two moving zazen.

Beats getting slapped with a bamboo stick in some
Ashram on Venice Boulevard

DETERIORATING

A piece at a time and urban leprosy losing pieces of my
psyche.
Happiness gone into the sink with pieces of gray and
white beard.

Peace of mind in a puss heap of gauze dropped into a
Hefty bag that already holds pieces scraped skin,
a shard of beard and skin poorly shaved,
sore throat, cannot swallow,
pulled a muscle showing off in the weight room
spilled some energy drink on the kitchen floor, and threw
out an old fish sandwich, I hoped to snack, at night, since
I cannot sleep as
three neighborhood pit bulls growl at 3 am,
I hear daughters arguing with their mother into the night
and across the street, some girlfriend offers to the night
"so you fucked me and now it's over, really ? really?
Jonathan
Dogs, daughters and lovers

And ceiling looks back, knowing what I am thinking
that there is an island somewhere were lepers decay with
dignity unlike here where each lost part is
laughed at and ridiculed and

yelled about leaving parts of you in that plastic bag from
7/11
and the mirror knows, as it X rays you, it is all bone and
flesh
powered by a spirit too bold or stupid to yield to the
deterioration.

TABLE 52

After a summer rain, clouds would thin, revealing a view
to the George Washington Bridge ten thousand city lights,
below, empty office buildings, red backup lights snaking
out of the city.

And everything glittered red, orange, white twinkles of
light reflecting up towards table 52

Here atop the World Trade Center overlooking everything
of value to this deal making world

When I came here it was for some big play or player,
women or work, and for an Andrew Jackson,

the maître d would maneuver me to this spot where big
plates and small portions open the way to odd and old
wines, from Hungary,

and a hand under the table,touching

some smooth thigh, concealed by a proper working
woman's black dress

there were always things to follow, deals, contracts, with
large hipped executives, with 5th avenue perfumes, Wall
street stares, and a giddy laugh.

Windows of the World glee, from this place, blazing white
tablecloth, marble floor

Turned into a killing field, rubble to dust, cluttered with
parts of people ripped apart by a Muslim lunatic

Living in a cave, reading the Koran, finding his hate of
modernity, the pretext to force innocents to jump out this
building to certain death
These enemies of modernity
Slayers of peace
Destroyers of beauty
Everything from Table 52 now memories distant
Replaced by nightmares, dust covered
Tears for every soul lost and every heart broken
And they read the names
Remember the good times
When all you could see from table 52 was the good life

LOOKS

Don't matter much, even most men think they do

Dicks matter some but not their size to most women who only want to make you limp anyway

In bed and out

You can get dropped handsome or gnarly

Long nosed or stout

Money means more, stature, and

Mostly devoted to making her happy and listen

Well to all of the stories of in laws and friends

An avalanche of woes from every place about everyone

Enough of her perfumes, shoes, clothes, therapists, plural

And those who hear it all and nod do better than the rest

Who are more fascinated by her thighs, lips, and that warm canal

Frictionville that takes money, time, and drama to get a roundtrip ticket to anything with her

Looks don't matter, never did

All those oohs and aahs, of slick cars and the smell of a crisp Franklin help but are not enough

It is attention,

lean in, and throw some Tahitian pearls around her neck from time to time

The face matters to you, not her.

EPISTEMOLOGY

Points to the origin of knowledge
How the cosmos and ideas hang from spoken word to text
from the disciples of Christ through
Kant to Hoffer, Hobbes, Sartre' and those other brains,
even Diderot.
Enlightened like Locke and Rousseau, hoping to find the
source of it all, what it all means,
Epistemology
Freud searched for it, in dreams and Id, through a cloud
of cocaine
Jung saw a collective consciousness, talked it through in a
stone cottage on some Swiss lake
Others have drank, fucked, and written themselves silly to
find that core of what we know
Or mostly do not
The source is somewhere, within or cosmic
How did they figure it all out or not
Don Juan had it right
Shaw knew
Wake up in silence, not to barking dogs
Eat well, shut up once in while, walk somewhere alone, get
rid of your attachments

Pause before you drop an opinion, criticize, or say you are
in love
Then it may come to you, what it is all about
As if you care

ENOUGH BEER

Head in the toilet bowl retching a 24 ounce of Foster's no
less
Ass water lapping against this old nose, longer now, aged
Taken in enough beer to bobble away
fart away another life disaster
Attempting to fill that wide emotional hole, 24 million
square kilometers across, as big as the hole in the ozone
Hoping that Blue Moon, Bud and Sam Adams will sew
up the loss of another woman, another one tossed you out
for being an old bore
The toilet water reflects a retched reflection of one who
has lost his youth and his allure
A lined face of loss and the bowl knows its deposits of
innards and ale that this is the bottom
By morning a new hope will rise, from an ever empty bed
Now it is but gag and spew to a calm exhaustion
The beer filling nothing but the bowl.

BALL AND CHAIN

There are long lines of us

Chained gangs

Workers shackled to places of varying dimension

Metaphorically

Watched by shotguns and whips

Who watch our overtimes, vacation days, consumption of
coffee, cups, paper and Danish

And we shake the bush to piss, and yell Yes Boss

Some of us think we are free

And some us think we are doomed

And most of us know we're here for all the wrong, weak,
unimaginative reasons, to

Pay the bills, the mortgage, for school, and to keep the
missus from shutting us down or off

And mostly just to stop the shouting

It is quiet on the chain gang, there is a groan, the clank of
your ball and chain

You get used to carrying the ball, shuffling and asking
permission

Cool Hand Luke it,

Break away, fight it out

And don't dig your own grave

BRAVE ONES RUN

Better to risk starving free

Than paying your Amex bill on time

There was fall in the wind, even here there are seasons,
imperceptible some years
Warm enough by that bay to strip down and change
behind a towel
Head out for a slow run into a fall breeze,bare chested at
noon.
Dogs chase Frisbees, a kayaker fights the current, and
flashes a white, white toothed grin,
Two women bikers pass me in high gear, wiggling hard
glutes and roped hamstrings
And today I glide for a while, turn car ward
A note is there under the wiper
Usually bad omens, a mad OCD guy, who hates that you
parked outside a line, a Thai menu,
Or some other irritant
This from woman in a white Porsche, driving away
It says she was impressed by my classic face, the resolve
to run,

But it is nothing more, but a fancy invitation to a yoga
class
Not to lunch or dinner
Or bed
Still it carries me through an otherwise tiring,
standard day
Amazed someone, especially a woman, even after my
money, appealed to
My vanity
Knowing men she does
Vanity, Ecclesiastes knew, is eternally
All of it
Vanity all is vanity
And a striving after the wind.

LOOK UP

I have never met a man

Who did not have downs and ups in life

Most have more downs of no fault of their own

Circumstances, bad luck, the forces,

Just the forces take you over, inexorably

Towards a result you do not want but cannot seem to

avoid

Then there are those who fly high on innate gifts, then

spend a lifetime

Destroying themselves on women, dope or both

Creating a spiral so strong and powerful they generate

their own vortex of trouble

All their gifts, joy, is crushed, by this self created sorrow.

A few emerge reborn after years of tumult, seeking

absolution from anyone who will

Give it

Mothers, wives, children

Often in tears from some epiphany, recovered from

cocaine or worse, or out of jail after some beef

All on restart, cleansed by their travail, and expecting the

rest of us to take something from it about

Second chances,I suppose

"Look up, Get up, and never give up"
Michael Irvin said, persist, insist, and resist
What is out there after you, chasing down and tracking
the good in you.

OLDER MEN

Talk less and rarely
Except to clerks, life of language in retreat
Nodding to family, neglecting and avoiding friends
Disengaged, rhetorically, any nuance of thought and
philosophy chambered
Inside slight movements of meaning, symbolizing
paragraphs of any triumph or remorse
Silently
Misplaced that soapbox, to shout out policy, politics,
imperatives, child rearing tips, discipline,
Art, and movements
Quiescent now, not forgetful or dissipated,
Orator without audience in a silent soliloquy to an
unseen mob
Are you so wise that you do not speak, or cannot
Tired of pronouncements, arguments without substance,
points of views on pointless things
Marcel Marceau of these later years, a mime of existence
Acting without dialogue,making no points, stirring no
crowds,
Simply mumbling in a garden to the trees, and falling
leaves

WHERE IS THIS SPAULDING GRAY?

Anyway

Out for a long swim to shore on Long Island sound or back in Indochina

Arm over arm in a warm Asian sea, with Cambodia dead ahead

Or on a stage, with a lamp and a chair reviewing his other life, before a mini van caught his rented car on a mysteriously dark night and shattered his hip, broke his skull, sending him into a Neolithic cave of depression, excruciating pain, and doubt that he had anything left

Onto another journey, this to an island of catatonics, and left him to curse the plate in his famous brow, search for bridges to jump, streams to swim in fully clothed.

Without a note or quarrel, he evaporated from wife and children, the brightest lights of his tormented life, left without a fatherly stare, searching they all did

By the dumpster on Broadway, behind the counter at Papaya, he is out there, damaged,perhaps but free, of the pain, searching for his old self, and the answer to the Big Me, of what life is about

Always that

Too much to endure, no retributions, everyone
understands, no need to exit stage right
Always you have a story to tell, even this one. Come back,
it will be just fine.
Swim home, man, swim home.

YOU CAN

Always walk the boards to Margate

Take in the sea breeze, hear the gulls cry

Watch a babe walk on too high heels, as her high

backside, rolls beneath an orange bikini

You can always do that

Sit in your 200 square feet room and smell the salt air on

everything, nap on damp sheets, and dry off with a wet

towel

Watch Balboa fight Creed to a draw for the hundredth

time, at 3am

Mouth every word of Godfather, and be Michael as he

settles with Hyman Roth, kills Fredo, and then put your

kitchen knife into Don Ciccio, who murdered the Don's

father.

By six the sun returns, and out there honor, retribution,

defending the family, are too much to ponder, on the

boards, old men walk and amble with a morning cigar

hanging out the right side of their mouth,

Young women jog and talk, the old ones sit on a bench

and watch the waves,

And you can wonder, too, are you just another bum from

the neighborhood afraid to step up

Or just too tired to go another round?

ASTERISK

You can hit homeruns over scoreboards
Past foul poles into the water at San Francisco Bay
Overtake even the babe, his swats, and Aaron's power
shots with a short
Super fast swing, not classic or pretty to observe in a slow
mo machine
You can swing for hours in practice
Hold back your hips, open them slowly, force
concentration, synchronize eye and hand
Even when 755 comes your way some sunny day at the top
of the second in SafeCo
And you causally send it to the opposite field
There are a few cheers, some boos, a sigh of relief and your
315 pounds round the bases
And only you know how much juice it took to get there or
didn't
Give the boys in the bleachers as much as they want and
see if they could hit the ball at all
You need skills, big league skills to hit 755 and .500
Enough of the hypocrites and pundits and beer fueled
critiques
Put that asterisk in some book, but forget the Hall of
Fame

755 is Everest of bats and balls, some use oxygen to get to
the top, some don't
A summit is a summit.
Screw the asterisk
A muscled, talented man named Bonds, batted one to
Kingdom Come and stands up for 756
So let him

MARX AND NOT KARL

It was a simple dialectic, Hegelian in design
For every thesis Karl was about in 1848 that intellectual
freeloader who mooched off Engels
Marx Toys was not in 1970
At 5am, we all showed up at the Erie plant
The foreman stood outside that summer and declared,"its
90, I need 90"
That's because it was that inside, few could make a full
eight hour day
There we assembled plastic dolls and horses, one toilet for
men, two for women, allowed ten minutes a dump or lose
an hour of pay
How did Karl miss this place. An old fashioned
sweatshop, that could not ever earn me enough to pay the
rent, a place to be until that real job came along.
So I counted out horse head, and those for dolls. Climbing
to boxes stacked 50 feet high, to bring these heads to
an assembly line of women, with anarchy far from their
minds, not a Norma Rae to be found.
Lunch was talk of pussy, intercourse, conquests, sodomy,
the women in aisle five.
Was this the conversation at the Shirtwaist factory before
the fire; of the peasants as they stormed the Bastille,
did Robespierre contemplate who he might lay during

the Terror. Did they discuss ass, once they looted the
Romanoff's castle and sent them to be shot.

10,000 horse, 15, 000 doll heads everyday, all summer 90
in 90. Two degrees, a college teaching post, and a summer
to kill being part of the proletariat .

Every wide eyed, wild ass college radical should man this
line, at this Marx place one summer

It enlightens one, the hard way

Climb the boxes, man the assembly line, talk cock and
pussy until you can't stand it, and then see where you are
when the "revolution comes

AND THESE ARE THE BUMS?

For 2 or three miles along the ocean walk there are clumps
of homeless, distressed, some with lost minds, people here,
the world calls them bums, the homeless, the wretched
By day break some have cracked a paperback, other just
lean on a very full backpack, others roll under stained
blankets, or a curl into a grease scarred sleeping bag
A few scream at daybreak, and shove over what is left of
a McDonald's breakfast,with only a half eaten sausage to
consume
An Asian fellow unfurls 20 paintings, and collects water
for another afternoon of creation, nearby a bearded tall,
thin man, curses the ocean, " he fucked me over.. I tell
you.. he fucked me over"
And a woman, does yoga on a mat, in layers of clothes, 6
coats thick. She disrobes slowly and silently stretches as
the old man curses, the Asian puts a stroke on his sheets,
and another eats that sausage slowly.
Different are they so much from the lunacy in the towers
above the, from the latex mob with crooked arms sipping
something, and talking about, what, all morning. Is one
judging the other?
There is for both a daily ritual, a recovery from their
drugs, booze, and life, directed or aimless

By the ocean, they occupy prime space, where there is
good light, passing time, if we could chose this, how sweet
a repast?
It is wasted, yet not ignoble
Give Brenda a brush, Valentine a blanket, Donald a meal
And stop judging

EFFORTING

Too much huffing and puffing
Far too much yearning and striving
Efforting

After, slimmer bodies, bigger biceps, tighter asses, white
teeth
Is the bird into the wind
The dolphin in a rough sea
The lion chasing prey
Efforting?

We have lost our nature, struggling with this way of
things trying
To mold what is slipping away and will be lost anyway
Every resolve to perform towards some resolution, to solve
and better
Us, all with substantial effort

Is more not done with enthusiasm, some joy, heartfelt and
complete, less strained or forced
Flow matters, more and can triumph
Resolving to just do and be
And leave effort and exasperation to others.

The more we strive, the more resistance grows
With resistance our path to our goals are altered
Everything becomes more difficult
And uncertain
Overcome, effort
And go with the flow

SUNDAY WALK

Crew cut lawns catch a morning dew

Aromas rise with humidity, blossoms and grass smells

Overtake the stench of high priced droppings from

standard poodles, retrievers,

Akita's

All left behind to simmer throughout the day by the same

selfish bastards arguing at each other

In their million dollar mortgage homes

She yells

"I will make an appointment, hey you bastard talk to me"

He says

"make a fucking appointment for what?"

She says

"don't pretend you bastard, you fucking bastard"

       He leaves

A new grey BMW pulls around a corner, the owner will

not leave the car, and coaxes his dog

"it's ok, sweetheart, its ok"

The dog crapped in his new back seat, and he shovels it

onto the grass, with the STYLE portion of his

       New York Times.

A quiet homeless man starts beating his one piece of

luggage with a stick, attempting to exorcise some evil

presence

Two brothers trim a hedge, laugh at how uneven it is. A neighbor offers them a beer at 8:30 which they take and swig,

As a realtor, in a smart yellow dress pushes a sign into a nearby lawn, and then picks up a pile of crap on the house lawn she hopes to show and sell. She smiles at the hedge cutters who raise their beers to her and clink them in a morning salute.

Flies gather at the park, hovering over a half eaten burrito, morning cursing turns silent, the curtain closes on Sunday morning, revealing another August afternoon.

NEWSMAN CIRCA 1976-77

In his right hand lower drawer there was whiskey and in
his upper left a carton of camels, filters.

And he ran a newsroom in Detroit like he ran his squad in
Korea, kick ass, with an occasional pat on the shoulder .

So when Jimmy Hoffa went missing, he worked us long
and hard and when we had a good showing, he asked us
in and lay out six shot glasses, and this squad would gulp
them down

Victory and a laugh and a smoke

Friday he'd take us to a Mexican place, ply us with tacos
and such and mostly pitchers of Sangria. And then he
would see if we could create a newscast in two hours and
high,

and we did always

He loved the news life. He rarely saw wife one or two,
or even three. During the Livernois riots, he forgot his
anniversary. By 2am he drove home, up the driveway
and heard glass breaking, and the faint smell of filet.
Under the wheels was a complete dinner, tablecloth,
candles plates and filet. And his clothes were piled on the
lawn in a heap.

Not as much anger by his wife as outrage and just hurt

He sorted through the Gucci shoes, the 100 dollar ties,
and salvaged what he could, including the marriage,when
she opened the door that morning.

He had a marriage, the riots, a town that was the murder
capital, Hoffa long gone, and his newsroom.

Nobody divorced him this time, and everyone appreciated
a place where guts, fairness, and being flawed seemed like
more than enough to get you through.

More than enough

FOOTBALL MAN

This guy was teamster, he owned trucks
You would never know it, at 6' 3" in an Italian silk suit,
grey tie and slicked back hair
Trucks brought big cash from deal makers some maybe
mobbed up, guys with thick hands and necks
But he was not a patsy for anyone and he gave as good as
he got
Enough cash to buy the Eagles, this guy most called
Leonard
To me Mr. Tose

He had a whole team to guide, mold, break if need be
But he loved his people, raised money for to fight
leukemia in kids
Every year had a picnic for everyone, never missed
showing up

At lunch he asked for 3 shot glasses and the waitress bent
low, so he could see her assets
"yeah honey, the regular, one for appetizer, the main
course and desert"
She poured Johnny Walker in all three,
and when I finished salad, pasta, and a slice of spumoni,
he drank the shots.

Between glasses he revealed, philosophy, some bullshit,
and a fair amount of angst over the
Bastards he could not charm, mostly the guys who held
his casino markers
Not me, he had me after the first shot.
You can trust a guy in a silk suit, who only has Jack for
lunch
With bruised knuckles and calloused palms

THE RAINBOW SIGN

What is it about that colored arc suggesting solace, peace,
beauty
Whether over sea or concrete, barrio, or mansion tall
Cars stop, people shutter at it,
Children go silent, couples embrace
Noah saw it first across the horizon that he thought he
would never see again
Dove with branch in beak
Noah mumbles to his son
No more water, the fire next time
As long as there are rainbows, we go on, is the myth of
it all
When I see one hope returns

WHAT IF'S

Eventually, inexorably, the what if's of a life stop clouding
the mind
No longer commanding the inner dialogue, that speaks to
what we might have done or been
Backward thoughts losing their power
It is enough to move forward
The rumble is the here and now and it shakes you awake
from a restless rest
And you rattle, at the unknowable, next
Taking a step anyway towards something
Another disruption from a rutted path of some comfort
if of no value to anyone
Disruptions, an affront forcing you to do something
unexpected
That might unnerve, stun and pull you somewhere you
are afraid to go
And you go, no more what if's, no more time for them

IMPOSTOR

Too many pretenders in town

Too many poseurs, fakers, without snake baskets, but are

snakes, all fakes

No Ganges secret water cures

So stuck on getting read, heard, or seen. Pushing on

phone, email, at parties, puffing up to be

Noticed

Validated

Recognized

Resurrected

Saved

Impostors we've become, to avoid facing ourselves.

Authenticity lost to survival,

survival killing the authentic.

All of it, shoving us away from whoever we were or are.

The why's we wrote, stocked, filmed, and spoke

Truths

Now lost to crippled souls, messaging each other and

everything from latte to brushing teeth

More energy on purity, unruffled, un puffed

Will outlast tom foolery, and all those barrel chested liars

with two chins, who say they know

Everyone and, you know, they know
Nothing

Impostors claiming value, running three card monte
games with your life
Follow your own path, create your game, impose your
authentic self on these charlatans
And evaporate them

RED SKY

If you let it, the sky can make you cry
The sun sinks revealing a yellow wash across the Pacific
Salmon colored clouds arise firing the horizon
Winds blow the clouds and the glow turns salmon to red

The 405 slows, necks turn right and left
The brave pull over, exit, snap a picture

I head to El Segundo, park, sit on the hood
Red sky burning, a Rothko canvas, vast, available to all
A grand democratic offering from the universe to us,
As though we might deserve it,
or earned it somehow

Eyes close and bright red is all my brain can see
Transported, to a softness and vulnerability, needed to
pierce this external,toughness crap

Red sky penetrates, illuminates, and melts the hard outer
crust of me to bring a tear.

PHILOSOPHERS AT THE ROLLER COASTER

There they are two,otherwise, homeless men, huddled under a ledge by Rubio's, a hundred feet from that old wooden roller coaster at Belmont Park.
Coney Island by the cleaner sea, not the Atlantic, and not Brooklyn
I am stopped by the light, and wisdom comes from a curb

"anything for me, buddy"

"If I had anything I' d give it to you, I'm running"

Then I tell him, it's been a bad day of cramps, too many phone calls, texts from everyone on and on

"There are no bad days man, you have it all dude" says the first

"you have all your hair, you're together my man, together" says the second

And before the light changes, I concur in their optimism as they share what is left of a reefer

Becket dialogue on a street corner,
across from the oldest wooden roller coaster, and it rattles
as we talk, rumbles

Two men waiting for something to get them through, no
ephemeral Godot, just me, with empty pockets to their
Estragon and Vladimir.

More wisdom here than most boardrooms.

THERE IS NO QUIET
HERE ANYMORE

Anywhere

Silence stolen by barking dogs, every neighborhood a
kennel

Pitbulls, Dobermans, even Collies

Dogs of the afraid, protecting little yards, behind
expensive, neat little shacks across West LA,

Gnawing at serenity, growling over birdsongs, yapping,
snapping, howling

At every natural motion even at a once quiet dawn

Who will poison them with rat pellets

Turn their dogs on them to eat them alive like the pigs of
the Dark Ages during the plague

Paying off the mortgage, 25 years still left, hoping for one
Sunday morning, just one a month

When all the dogs sleep late, or are dead

I'M NO DALAI LAMA

I met him once, the Dalai Lama along the Wasatch range
in the valley of the Mormons
Far from his temples and Indian enclave
His presence made all serene and balanced for a moment
even though he talked of suffering and life, he
offered the Buddha's way out of it, this life of struggle
Not having any of his lineage, or being anywhere evolved
as high on the karmic ladder,

Without robe in modern dress
Accept
Identify with the outcast, and pariahs,
study heretics and rebels,
travel outside the comfortable roads,
defy the status quo, read what is forbidden,
if anything still is,

Be still on occasion, silent totally, defy scandal and the
short cuts, they take you on a long road anyway
Hold onto your sanity and
lean against the great wall of what is, until it falls over, so
you can step into what can be, and run
through the high grass

Build your own paths, bushwhack through life's jungle,
trek to your Loch, Castle and horizon
And mostly forget what you can,
the purely bad knotted ugly things of life like it is, and
stupidity, and missed chances,
and remember

Whatever lessons you have grabbed from any success and
more failures, sweet failures that provides more, much
more for good effort
In one deep Zen breath, know this
Only follow a path that has heart
Your heart
Amazing what an audience with the Dalai Lama does for
your perspective.

SOMETIMES YOU ARE
IN A SPOT SO PURE
YOU CANNOT MOVE

A small swallow of a Coke sitting in a plastic chair, facing
the Pacific,
commanding from this sandy deck
that you have reached that spot on the life wheel where
you are about to move somewhere, but
You cannot move

Fearing the next moment
will be in horror working back to this ant, wasp, or you
return as an unattractive Russian babushka, or worse the
mole on her cheek
So you dare not move

Even after some time with that someone,
a warm sweet calm, where time is gone, holding each
other starring at nothing, thinking of nothing,
ecstasy, without argument, fury or desire or even
judgment

And you do not want to get up to lose this spot, so pure
you cannot move
Counting to 1,000 to 10,000 to 50,000 before you move
Knowing you must, afraid of what comes next, hoping
you will return to this and the world will stop again

EVERYONE GETS LAID TONIGHT IN PHILLY

This never happens
Not in Philly
Where everyone runs up the Art Museum steps, all 72 of
them, since Sly birthed Rocky
Where on most Sundays, they eat cheesesteaks, munch
soft pretzels with mustard
All the clichés of tough guys in hoodies and green parkas,
roaming through South Philly by the Vet, wanting the
Iggles to win again, go the distance, to have Super Bowl
dreams, great coaches like Vermeil,
Grown men fantasies, seen across ice cold turf, snow
plowed parking lots and wind chilled stands,
Reid, Lurie, number 5, finalize it, toss it, win it, a single
victory that sends them hurtling towards the big game.
Everyone roars until they cannot speak, hoarse now, 70
thousand of them

With one spirit, Philly wins a playoff and Marty, Jacko,
Tony, James and Jefferson will all get laid, finally. From
the same gals who never said hello on Sunday or ever
whispered in their ears or anywhere

One chance for a happy night without rancor or silence or arguments revisited
A simple lay for one victory, where both are few and far between.

I WOULD RUN AWAY

If I had some place with palm trees,
turquoise lagoons,
white sand, outside some hut where I could open the day
with 600 strokes out and 600 back

Instead of this one room
With a bed someone else owned
On borrowed pillows under a window where
The street sweepers come each Wednesday at 5am

There is nothing here
No hidden 15,000 page autobiography
Like Artie Shaw, no memorabilia of 8 wives
Pictures of them, memories of romance, then dissolution
and passionate nights
Not here

A few notebooks of bad poetry
Sorrow between blue lines
One old X-rated gallery under the bed
An old Navy knife that now cuts oranges not throats,
two pairs of shoes, some suits, a belt only one

There are no steps to a tropical lagoon, no red dirt back
roads to some French seafood place, all of that Gauguin
memories, only that

I want to run to them, leave the bill for college tuitions
The marital fights, the long unbroken silence of a life
stopped
Gone cold and dark, withering, into this shivering, frail,
body that cannot find its way to the toilet in the dark at
4am, or is it
A destiny still buried out there by that palm tree, where
the warm wind still blows and beckons
That but arriving there, all is well
And the search is over

VAN GOGH SAYS....

You have to eat well

Be well housed

Have a screw from time to time

Smoke your pipe and drink your coffee in peace

He was neither crazy nor obtuse

Offered something to the world

That only he could see and gave it the rest of us

SOMEDAYS YOU ARE

Invisible

No one sees you

No one speaks to you

Floating from one space to another at some 7/11 in a car

to a lonely road

At 117 mph in the desert

No one in the rear view mirror

No one to pass

Hit the button, invisible and spin out 5,000 rpms to

Zabrieskie Point

And up that slope

Speechless, solemn

You sit and stare over millennium of erosion and layers of

time

Tan, white landscape

That is precisely your feeling of how nothing matters

Nothing

Everything finds its level

Low, sanded terrain

Eventually all peaks are rounded, all shapes washed out

Canyons cut

And it is your portrait this view of it

Worn, rutted, 5 million years of rain, wind, leaving this

Quiet place that survived

Everything

Who else has seen you in that morning reflection

Lines, lost hair, larger brow eroded by time, molded by life
and genome

Lines of pain, some joy, quiet features, with no overlook in
some desert for others to view you

The desert stares back at you

Through you, another passing face etched by life

Mostly invisible in the desert night

ONE OILY BROWN BAG

Stained from within by a remnant of an egg salad
sandwich caught between a piece of wood and the curb,
decaying under the southern California sun, inches from
its end, gutter bound
Inside that bag I am feeling
Discarded, festered, gone,
awaiting a tube of rubber and steel up my ass, in search of
lumps of flesh
Everyone is cheery, seen enough assholes, clipped a jiffy
bag of polyps from old men dying eventually anyway
Others seeking clearance to go back to their cigars, and
marbled steaks. And then a brief chat with a soft face, out
of focus, a long haired nurse named Marna
Twilight sleep leaving medical, philosophical, political
riffs silent, until recovery, and then the world returns
Clean, enough, for now, it seems, nothing seen, clipped, or
altered.
Tortuous colon, he says
Right like life, I mutter to no one
The chemistry set of my life does not show up here, at this
scoping, it will take a deeper probe
Mood elevates after any procedure, the oily bag gets
kicked to the drain,

off to the ocean

Towards the clean surf, as young men on boards, not
anticipating the day when they will lay on their left side,
hoping for nothing more than a few more years to play at
life.

EVIL IN THE WORLD

Often comes embodied, not conceptually, euphonic,
figurative,literal
In flawed bodies, unheroic in shape, with voices of various
timber with
Ticks, quirks, distorted limbs, humps, squint eyes, fat lips,
thick waists, and full of hair
All burning from within to alter the way of all things, to
turn their way
Crooked

History serves them up, after pauses, without them, they
return often easily discerned, but as often tolerated, too
long
Until they unbalance the scales of what we can accept
besides just, injustice
Turquemada cut out intestines, boiled them in oil, ripped
off limbs and scattered them
Evil limited by technology
Hitler, Mussolini, Stalin killed more with less effort

UBL and his destroyers of modernity, murdered for the
distorted view of Allah, and beheaded and aimed planes at
innocents for the Koran says so

Tortured minds, texts and evil acts again. Men who must die to free us of their black hearts and souls

Different not from men in white collars using hierarchy and power to defile and destroy, while the white robe watches from a balcony

All evil is the same

Seen too late, after it hurts too many

Until outrage mounts an offensive

Until the forces overtake them

Never soon enough, or ruthless enough, too detached from it, until

Too many broken children, entire generations lost to bad intentions

Will to power, dominance, single minds of hate

We must kill them and send their spirits to dark space or shutter at their return

Kill them or they kill us, or worse so damage us we forget what evil is

Evil always loses, at what cost?

POPCORN

Who was that asshole who put popcorn in movie theaters
It's gulped in handfuls, gnawed at by the beaver people
always behind you
Meticulously masticated one kernel by one kernel in front
of you
Slurped with butter to your right
Lost in a noisy bag to your left
Now supersized, dripping in oils
Couples waddle into seats, so ready to devour
Crackling, smacking, distracting
Carefully crafted dialogue lost, tears caught, to this
popped maize
Nothing Bogart or the Duke could survive, only Rocky
and Skywalker
Give the next Noble and lifetime achievement award to
the guy who creates the silent kernel
That even the biggest slob can't smack, pop, or swallow
whole.

NANCY FIVE HUSBANDS

She looked new, all over, at 50 with a slim neck, hallowed
cheeks and rouge
After five husbands, she went through enough money to
pay off her mother's house in West Palm
Her hair had that blonde highlight tint against an auburn
mane that all the society dames at the Trump Tower wore
Everywhere else she was aerobic thin and firm

As I raised my head from the Waldorf salad, at the
Waldorf
there were her perfectly round 34's, bright teeth, and
emerald eyes, brought on by contact lens
Every husband gave her something
Breast job
Butt and tummy tuck
A smooth neck
Veneers of Oscar night size

Where was that actual girl next door, who took off her
clothes for boys in her garage by the breezeway?
The same girl whose brother hit me in the head with a bat
at 12, swelling my brain
Nancy five husbands with all her additions, natural
and not

Holding my wrist in a tight grip, wanting, perhaps,
something not provided by the others

A kind word, a memory of youth, a simple complement, a
kiss on soft lips from one adult to another
Or just to see Nancy across that table before the lifts and
expensive tucks, without judgement or pause
A girl from the neighborhood, with a broken heart.

EVEN THE GANGSTAS SMILE

Dark sky over this Thanksgiving, gray, damp air, no sun on any exposed necks

But it not a work day, so

Even the Gangsta's smile,, with tats exposed from neck to waist, with broad smiles
to go with their bravado,
As the swing from ring to ring, like monkey's on an outing at muscle beach, near the Santa Monica Pier

Like every one else more or less casting away everything else, even shirts, and have the sea breeze bite into their exposed skin
Red bikinis cannot hold those long tan breasts on the brunette who speaks an Eastern European tongue, as the boys from the hood talk her up in Spanglish
Two almost naked teenage girls attempt to maneuver a bike for two on the strand to poor effect, but no one cares their thongs the only focus as they pedal by
20 hairless, bare chested, college boys play what passes for Rugby,
as a youngster of six or eight cries for a lost father, who is only lost in reverie watching the thongs go by

Enough thanks to go around, especially to the couple
making out in the Benz back seat, with his bare ass in the
air and only the soles of her feet signifying her presence
Then there is sun, finally
warmth on my neck, everyone seems benign, wholesome
and free, the knives on their belts are sheathed, and even
the gangsta's smile.

CONTROLS

You can brood, clench teeth, scream into the Detroit night
Go on long walks when the stars are gone, crush a few
roaches, stomp ants, or pull moths apart
Cry alone, where else?

As you sit in your one chair at 3am
Nothing will suddenly control the chaos real or not that is
your perceived existence
You can plan, stare at the ceiling for guidance, hope for
intervention from the cosmos
Read a few Stephen Covey books, throw in Marianne
Williamson, who wants to be President now

Talk to your coach, counselor, or therapist. Text them, if
you are beyond utterance
Even attempt to console with the current female avatar
Pray for it, meditate at it, pine on it, see your future, create
a damn vision board of pictures from magazines
You cannot subvert or convert the forces that be, or the
train of destiny barreling towards your chest
You can control what you think
How you fill your mind, with crap and noise or not
What you put into your pie hole that honors or defiles
that body

And control what the hell comes out of your mouth.

What you say, that can soothe, elevate moods or pollute everyone and everything

It is all about choice, buddy, the rest

Is just cosmic bull,

from quantum powers I do not get, and cannot know with any certainty

It is otherwise all random, loose particles, unbound by my thoughts, words, and deeds

Get real control of what you can

What I think, say and consume,

Will not rock the universe, but it will get me through and you through a day

ONE ARMED BOY

On that bench in the gym who has slowly lifted on
each machine, to bring his frail body to a manly form,
adjusting each weight,
Carefully attempting to not appear self conscious about
that right arm gone at the elbow
This son of someone's sorrow with green eyes and a
Marine brush cut, enough courage to just go on, expose
himself to the self absorbed, hair bags of various flab and
missing sinew
Eyes down,bench to shower, wounded somehow by fate
twisted to hurt this boy, surrounded by pot bellied,
toweled men, dedicated to their vanities, not a smile or
emotion from him, or them
One day I will say hello, to let him know he is stronger,
much stronger than the rest of us

THE UMPIRE RIDES A HARLEY

To a Sunday baseball game near the place where they
make movies and television shows
And across the road from a country club created by
Groucho and his Jewish buddies, they could play cards,
smoke, drink, and on occasion, golf
On this diamond, there are no Thalberg's, no Zeppo or
even a Warner brother's son, only working stiffs kids, and
fathers, looking for a morning away from everything, with
nothing more than a baseball coming their way, or hitting
a sweet spot at bat
Limbs are wrapped, wrists braced, that aroma of Ben Gay
fights the smell of freshly cut grass, and discarded beer
cans
A bad call at 2nd empties the benches, for about 5 seconds,
then the Ump shouts
"God damn it, its just a game, Christ Almighty"
And as quickly as they rose they retreat, the tempers of
these men, who spend the week containing emotions,
desires and all other passions are used to calming down
So the game goes on
With the gusto of men at play, abandoning the other
life for a morning of baseball with a middle aged, bald
umpire, declares

"red wins 6-4 have a great week"

Tucks his ball cap in his shirt, fixes his mask on the back
seat, quietly starts the 250cc engine, with a smile, and S's
his way out of the jammed parking lot, and by the time he
gets to the light, he's at 50, with a small breeze in his face.
A lanky pitcher, Jimmy Stewart type, offers to buy a
round of Bud, and he gets a half hearted cheer.
And someone at Hillcrest hits a golf ball over the fence,
and it bounces on the street, jumps over a black SUV, and
is chased by a gal jogging with her retriever.

SAY GOODBYE TO
JOHN WAYNE

Patriot, conservative, protean actor, unvarnished,out
spoken, star
Green Beret,
Sargent Stryker at Iowa Jima,
Ethan Edward in Searchers,
McClintock,
Rooster in True Grit

The Duke

In Orange County, near the place where he docked his
yacht, they named the airport after him in 1979, and put
up a statue to his name and essence.
Mostly, Republicans did it, because most of the folks in
that county then, were
John Wayne Airport for a man who sat with Nixon and
Kissinger, knew Reagan as a friend, and even debated
Harvard's best libs on Vietnam, 1974, to the Lampoon, he
offered:
"I am quite prepared to meet nose to nose and fact to fact
any or all of the knee jerk liberals who foul your campus"
He rode to the campus in an armored personnel carrier,
driven by Green Berets

Now they want the airport free of the Duke.
Because in a Playboy interview in 1971, he disliked
Easy Rider, Midnight Cowboy, gay men, affirmative
action, and anti Americanism
Howdy!
Pull down that statue, no need to celebrate his
accomplishments, he was a man of his time
so were Columbus, most of our Presidents, and a few
Generals
McKinley is gone, in Arcata, some Native Americans have
damned him for no reason
Columbus is painted red for genocide
Father Junipero Serra is decapitated for converting
indigenous people
So Orange County has changed, so has America, so what
A nation that has no past has no future
Will they dynamite Jefferson on Rushmore next
Stand by, pilgrim, it's crazy out there

SO YOU THINK YOU MATTER

There are enough egos, super egos and ids
Some Jungian shadows and archetypes to go around
Too much talk therapy, transactional analysis and
Cognitive behavior techniques to bend every mind on all
7 billion of us

Enough defensive moves to hold onto your purpose
Smoke screens of words, packed into missiles of anger
Puffed up importance and delusions of grandeur to go
around

As though it matters.

Your degrees, career notches on your belt of life,
the cash,
cars, diamonds, guns, gold stuff,
and pictures of exploits, suck ups, on your personal wall of
fame and acclaim

The Low Frequency Array will say, hold on, take a breath
Jose'
200 hundred astronomers just found 300,000 new
galaxies
Billions of light years away

Larger than our Milky Way
and here we are with our steel belted radials, AAA, unable
to afford our meds, fish tacos, and the occasional kind
word or touch, searching for what?
Their center, black holes, so immense, that never stop
eating, everything, eternally,
Non stop black holes

As we float through space, the entire galaxy of ours,
towards some cosmic demise
That has been delayed
Andromeda is coming 68 miles a second, gets here around
4.5 billion years from now
So get your affairs in order,
it is coming slower than they thought it has a 20 mile per
second drift
so that's another 600 million years extra,
If a single sentient anything is still here when Andromeda
arrives, maybe they will have figured it all out, made
some damn sense of any of it

CONSCIOUSNESS

This is one of the wonders
An internal thing, in our control, if we want to pilot it
That sense of who we are on any day
Unassailable, protected, unmoved

There is a knowing, an inner stability,
That only we can touch and allow to send us
Towards purpose, outcomes, and results
Always accessible

No need for excuse or complaint
Sarcasm and humor to avoid yourself
You have this, sanctum, but to go there
And rest up for next and to overcome not and never
Be responsible for your own consciousness
It cannot be directed externally
It is outlook, and mood, attitude and awareness
At one moment to the next

Do not give it away to the nag, the screamer,
Her legs and ass, the suited overseer, the intimidators
They can all be handled, beaten or destroyed

By what you know, that interior fortress of you, your sense of self

Always challenged, but resilient enough to overtake the forces
Quiet, pause, then act

POPS POETRY

Poems of roses and thorns
Birds that chirp at dawns light
Squirrels and rabbits
Poppy fields and violets

Women with Modigliani necks
Da Vinci smiles
Asses of Rubens
Naked, sensual women of Gaugin

Poets who whine and cry
Eloquence of love and loss
Unrequited episodes
Breaking hearts and twisting minds

There are no robins in my foxhole
No flowers in my tank
I have not seen a women or touched one in a year
I am eating MRE's, and trading, cigarettes, for a
Milky Way
Two clicks down the way, the guys I shot are piling up

It is bright and cold, in this desert country
Mountains of bad guys who quote Allah
And want me dead by night

I do not dream of women in clothes or not
Mostly think of sundaes, waffles, and Thanksgiving
And carry her picture, to remind me what I am supposed
to be fighting for

I am a poet I suppose, and they call me Pops, older than
the other guys
Caught in this life's trap.
Someday, I 'll write the other stuff of flowers, love, and all
But for now, it is not about heroics, just about looking out
for your buddies,
And promising yourself, you will make it home, somehow,
In one piece, if possible.

SNOW FALLS ON
TIMES SQUARE

spots of yellow dart down Fifth Avenue, cabs snaking over
plowed streets.
A few buses exhale stopping for a shivering pod of hourly
wagers who need the eight hours, 2 feet of snow or not

Out of the Queens apartment window. One son gazes out
over the city. He dare not enter
his cab buried lost in a 4 foot drift.

By an El Segundo beach. A father rides the rusty bike for
20 miles, passing bikinis and latex covered butts, pausing
for the sounds of surf, to watch.
A woman spreads Hawaiian Tropic on her legs, smelling
of the beach, lotion warms skin and she smiles.
All of it here in summer in January.

Sun ushers some bliss, as old Joe said, follow your bliss,
and here it is
momentary

Son sits in an old chair
looking out at snow gray Manhattan skyline
father on a towel playing 18

Quiet contemplation of snow eating up the rent
Of lotion on long legs in the sand

Both wanting each other as a snow falls on a central Park
path past the green tavern where they would talk over
coffee and eggs.

CLEANING NEW YORK

No place needs them more nor appreciates them less.
These cleaners and sweepers with mops and rags wiping
everything anyone touches,
sweats on
craps on
or kisses on.

Sweat faced people learning English, still laughing and
eating in between plugging in vacuums, collecting hair of
wealthy people, folding wet towels, scraping off gum.
Just cleaning for self centered ass holes everywhere.

What do they know on their knees and learned bent over
things that others miss
a city defiling itself at every tick-tock, generating refuse
and expecting someone else will pick up after them.

Grown-ups still children, unable to consider anyone but
themselves.

Inconsiderate,
filthy New Yorkers

being wiped clean by these hearty upturned faces.
These Zen monks of Manhattan offering only honest
labor channeling all the good they can through their wet
cloths and brooms

COAT AND TIE WORLD

In the elevator. There are classes Marxian in tone $50
haircuts and $1000 suits and $75 ties
close shaved corporate men pretending to be Marines off
to some fake battle of consumption for something
Warrior metaphors, battles of words and pen,
Their demons of their own creation not from Iowa Jima or
the Chosen Reservoir

Just three feet away silent and wistful painters, messengers,
flower girls with green pots and small women of Incan
descendent,
with pizza covers warming the pies of a conference room
full of attorneys who haven't picked up their own food
since Christmas.
In a real battle
I side with the tieless
the home haircut
the callused hand
give them a medal for honesty and Bronze Star and an oak
cluster
for getting up each day to ride those elevators with the
swells.

At least acknowledge them, consider opening a smile, a greeting
some justice to suggest for a moment that we are traveling together.
In this elevator that is our life.

YO HOT SHOT

With receding hair and puffy face. He looks like a comic or a jester.

He has a borscht belt smile and a firm handshake and a body of mush. There are handfuls of flesh to grab and a forest of black hair and a hint of perfume behind his ear.

And he has a popstar named Brittany in his bed, at 2 am, and her ankles, sometimes around his neck.

Hot Shot he is, owner of the entire place, from crap table to nightclub above the clouds, that rarely are there in this desert town
Could it be he gave her the entire 54th floor to play in in this casino that is his in Las Vegas.
When she wants to catch rays from a 103° sun, or have him spray some sunscreen on her back and undo the bra he sends for bulky men in black with gold chains, a diamond palm tree amulet around their necks and they close the doors and
the entire pool is hers.

He returns to his office, watches, as she wiggles in her bright orange suit and he has a rise there,

a warm rush travels to his brain, not bad, he thinks for a
guy leveraged to his eyeballs, near a fall,
enjoying it now, knowing his is a soul sold long ago to
someone, who is now, no one in particular.

I MISSED THAT WAR

through stupidity, not guile, thinking they only wanted
fighting men
so much else to do,
other things could have been,radioman, communications
supply and mechanic from chopper to rice paddy.
Other men were there and
I miss the war

Through honesty, not fear.
Lining up in my underwear barrel chested and seemingly
strong with some street scars from battles of my own for
nothing more than
turf and pussy.
Leaving gaps in bone and stitches on flesh and for that
I miss the war

The same 19-year-old faces, return there, some burned or
shot.
Still, I refrain from being there, unable to keep up or be
relied upon.
Unable to hold up a squad waiting for my head to clear or
these broken bones that have kept me away.

The Sgt. took me to an X-ray machine. After I had passed
the tests for officer candidate school
and when he saw them
he threw his head into his thick hands
came over to me and in a soft voice
"Sorry, kid, you are 4 F, that's it you're out"

And so I missed the war

Young and firm. I was 4-f'd

I did not avoid it, but I did not think it through.
Perhaps I could have
should have been there
and now still firm but too old to ride a tank to Baghdad.

Sitting in a chair, watching others again, always watching
others, in this sandstorm that is my life
where there are no Kevlar plates or IED's. Only the heat of
the moment.
The ongoing battle of life with its twists and regrets.

Wondering all the what if's and if true's
the now whats, and those heroic moments?
Would they have been mine. Could I have saved, someone
been victorious, a man of valor ?

All questions unanswered,

as are all regrets unresolved.

And what have I done with the life

Since I missed the war.

A MOUTH OF MANY COLORS

Many colored teeth in this mouth.
There were all these his teeth except for his upper
wisdom's that were pulled in a chair in Peoria before lunch
and bleeding into cotton balls returned to work.

The rest of varying color and hue off-white, yellow and
oyster caps in the originals mingled in this mouth that has
chewed in 15 cities,

Been hit in the mouth a dozen times. Once by a Marciano
right hook. When he wasn't looking. The mouth kissed a
few dozen women
sunk it into anyone he could find, each tooth story of
different colors.

Many repairs
Each place thereby some dentist of record on the dental
plan of someplace you worked for now forgotten.

And he told himself he would get them bleached white out
for uniformity and smile and manner,
but he has not stopped long enough and has lost a
whitecap or two swimming in Moravia or climbing
14,000 feet in Colorado.

What tests are there for someone's smile, who earned certificates in eighth grade for being the best at it, who barely smiles anymore at anything for anyone.

A multi-colored mouth hidden unlike Jacobs coat of colors not to be seen as the darkness within keeps the smile locked behind pursed lips.

I'M TIRED OF

All the tough guys who intimidate
scream
role play life like a B movie with their rules and moods
that we all put up with

They are the bosses of doom
turning our balls and pulling
knowing few will not follow at their every yank.
Masters of the current modern age and women as well.
Some harsher who talk of shoes with red soles, bad
moods,their underwear and less of what is at stake except
their own rising stars.

Men and women who want to be the big swinging Dick
And are constantly jumping in front of you waving their
dominance while you eat shit
chat or get in your car to go home.

The generation of workers from all other places, beaten
back by the proverbial buck and its quest, putting up with
anything and everything, just to make ends meet.

Bone weary, ready to retreat or fight back with anger. No.

The shield is within us, our protection, our own self-image. It cannot be penetrated, stabbed or strangled in less we let it.

EMPTY

You notice small things when your life is tumbling dry.
Nothing big at all.

She no longer smells of her favorite perfume . That
distinctive smell of her and the bottle in that place by her
mirror. It sits square and clear now
glass bottle empty, with no single dabs to place behind
her ear,

The bottle is abandoned. As is her heart for me. Once a
reservoir of good thoughts and yearnings.

Empty.

I wonder if it is unfilled because she wants no more
memories, no more caresses.

This mellow mist on her neck and by the inside curve
of her breasts once on the pulse of her wrists and how I
would actually swoon over it on her now gone with the
Paco Rabanne or the Calandra

Nothing left

So I might replace it grasping at the ring of eternal hope
that she will return it to her skin as a reminder of what we
once had.

Or just spray some of it on a small towel and keep it
with me like some Victorian sop. At least I will have it to
inhale. As the nights grow lonely as the years pile up.

All imagination none of it real anymore, years and years of
aromas that brought some comfort .
Now left to this small square towel, that may hold a
fragrance and memories for all the years ahead without
her and alone.

BATHROOM SURPRISE

Hellhole latrine with porcelain appliances made
ecologically sound without urinal wafers saving water.

I suppose so few places in LA like this or worse, a vast
coastal plain of men with cramps and bloated bladders,
hoping for some open pit by a tennis court, where
the Guptas throw back hands at each other and the
Goldbergs's hit forehands to the Chens and Kims.

Inside I go white-haired and hooded
attempting to look as threatening and solitary a force as
I can.
Nothing more than a void through a fog at 8 AM sucking
in the smells of lilacs and the purple haze of falling petals
of the Jacaranda.

Against the wall. A skeleton man stands attempting to
find the last notch on an ancient belt
skin gray as his beard
. Another lost one, lost soul,schizophrenic or just life
tossed. I empty into the waterless device. Only the sound
of the flow echoes off the dirty block concrete wall.

Pity rises and ends as the moment passes.

When the cell phone rings atop his backpack. Even he is connected to something to someone who may or may not know where he is leaning and how hard it is to find the hole in this belt.

And to whatever his world is
Inside his head and whoever is there.
The device lights his face and shirtless, he raises his chin and yells straight at me
"who the fuck is this"
Launched into the modern era in a latrine by the tennis court.
He may be disturbed or not, but there is a being there aroused by this phone of his. And for one moment, there is clarity out of his solitude and all I can do or want to do is piss.

MEN ALONE

At the deli on Ventura, they sit in small booths' holding
phones to their long lobbed ears
With hair in them, in all the wrong places out of ears and
nose,
Some together with other altecockers and altecrickers
Even together, they are alone, decades with one woman,
others with 2 old wives, who have thrown them away
like leftovers wrapped in foil, after years of love, children,
and even some of considerable fame

No complaints when she leased the Mercedes, the 30k bar
mitzvah for Brian, or took trips to Tellum and Belize.
Alone now with the steel rolled oatmeal, whatever the hell
that is and the dry toast.
Talking far too loudly to please the waitress in tight black
latex pants, of women who might blow them in their old
age, and not require
A checklist,
a flight plan of do's and don'ts, why do you's,
before they can enter her locked treasures,
and rise again these old hard men, with the occasional
hard ons.
No senior blues for these grey eyed wise men, unwilling to
trade a life of rules just to have morning wood.

A generation of men sipping egg creams, watching their cholesterol, so they can outlive the bitch who threw them away,

Alone, but unbroken,

these Kings of life, failures of marriage,

fathers of a lost brood, searching for some recognition that they have not erred, or stumbled on that well worn path, overcoming what passes for regret and sorrow with

A thick, hot pastrami, some ice cold,cole slaw, and the chocolate soda,

more seltzer than chocolate.

50 LAPS

By 40, I began running laps at the high school track on
my birthday
Every five years
At 50 it took almost 2 hours, each lap a year starting at 50
going backwards
Sounds easy, try it.

Adult, young married man, adolescent, headed backwards,
back to those beginnings, everything you tried to run
from, you are running towards, slowly coming to it at 40,
37, 25, 10, 5, birth
Each lap has its moment, it apex and apogee
1st fight...7
Kiss...9
Date...15
Sex of some sort 14, 15,....16
Divorce, kids, marriage, more kids, and divorce,
Some career success, plateaus, big jobs, bigger money, and
gone
Rebounds, dead children, lost parents, foreclosure
Loan paybacks, the no retirement blues,
All there lap by lap

Facing it five years at a time, on ovals of dirt, cinder, and
soft rubber, from one city track to another
One living biography, revealed, in sweat, wind, forcing
tears on some laps, you did not expect,
How long can it last, the years, the legs, the consequences
of life revealed, in the monotony of a birthday run.

I AM STARTING OVER

I told her, some large bosomed Italian gal who was an
expert in HR
Which meant nothing to me or her
How I roamed through malls just to see a movie at the
local Cineplex
Stayed all night one ticket, to not feel alone

Worked out at a gym with an overpriced membership
Ran hard, watched the teevees, observed strong women
sweating, without turn on or contact
No smiles not a nod of recognition, invisible

At work I was the oldest now, more chaperone than
colleague
Mentor and guide not equal anymore. All the guys I came
up with are dead or lost in Boca Raton with
their first wives.
Others took me off their lists, or stayed mad for some
unforgotten infraction, to them.

And the creditors only want their money.
Amex wants payment.
VISA and MasterCard something.

The hole deepens, as the cavity in my right lower molar taunts and robs of sleep. It's not about justice or right and wrong, it's more elemental.

Pay me.

So, I tell her. I am starting over. As far north and west as I can go, before Juneau, I laugh.

Dreaming of nothing, only reverie of warm southern California afternoons,

a fleshy brunette to caress under some star clear night,

and actually picking up a check somewhere, like Mastro's in Beverly Hills.

So I smile.

Politely,

at the HR gal at her 250 lbs, with her double D's, and wish her well as she does me, to her,

"give it time, you'll like it here"

Perhaps.

Another start over looms, south of somewhere, west of where I am.

BOX LUNCH MIRACLE

The cash dwindled by Tuesday, there was 9 dollars in my
right pocket, an expense check that I could not cash until
Monday
I parked in a garage that would validate a ticket after a
workout
Hunger actually came and ebbed between reps on the
Smith machine
Not much but enough to know,
there was an orange for breakfast, and some pretzels from
a saved bag
I do not remember being without food or wanting it more,
This was a real fast, not of Zen or faith, just hunger pangs,
that karmic payback for a run of bad picks

Thoughts of free bar food, came and guided me
towards one,
then, a white box appeared, a discarded box lunch.
And the universe, you curse, delivered a cookie, an apple,
and ½ of a vegetable sandwich.

Ate it . Slowly. Even offered a prayer on that rainy night,
hoping to send it to a star, the gratitude I had for this
offering from nowhere, and no one.
Everyone says take the chance, explore, leave your lane.

Next time, ask, Is there food there?
Or, will there be a box for you, with an apple and a half
eaten sandwich, when you can't cash a check,

and the dampness of bad choices runs through you,
on a Seattle night.

THE RAVEN KNOWS

Sits on a wooden sign
Making a turn off at 390' below sea level, he awaits cars
from
Arizona, Nevada, California carrying tourists searching
for views of things they cannot see back home.

Where their lawns are closely cut and their pools tended to
by olive colored boys carrying long white poles, so he sits
Moving a ravens head back and forth as a desert wind
parts the feathers on his neck
But only I appear without a crumb for him
Only a nod to this stoic form thinking..

It is probably some omen or an reincarnated Indian
warrior watching over
Zabrieskie Point waiting for all the white men to die away
and return it all to his slaughtered tribesmen
So.. it is quiet here

Even the raven does not crow
My deep breath, is the only sound
We stare at each other. Who knows more.

I have brought nothing here, waiting for a life sign,
Hoping to take something away, before this bird flies.

I want to become it, shape shift like Don Juan in a
Castaneda fantasy
Populate my warrior spirit, smoke peyote, merge with a
gorgeous Mexican women
Wing over the painted rocks, and shriek

Scream until the world seems sane

I AM DONE BACKING UP

To the tough guys in their pick ups with their pits and
Dobermans by their sides
These men who believe everyone is afraid of them, and
their thick forearms, hairy backs, and sharp toothed dogs.
I'm done listening to them
Imposing their code of might
Moral or not on everyone

You hear them yelling at clerks and their kids, at drive in
windows, their girlfriends, and grabbing other men by the
neck, too afraid to push them away
Hate these stereotypes, but there are some, enough of
them

Bullies of the modern age who have dogs for dicks, screw
hard, slap their kids around and piss off the rest of us
I am done with them, they give all of us bad names, make
good men suck ups all the same.

Rather nurse a broken nose, a cut lip or a sore hand than
let them tell me anything
It is not politics. The are from the left and right.
Done backing up, done listening to the boasts,

Time to take a shot back at them, declare any patch of
concrete free land
End of barbarism, triumph of civility.
Whether with fist or phrase, it is not only your way,
anymore.

MARCH MOON

The March moon illuminates. A cold blue light.
Casts enough brightness on an empty beach.
Moonshadows, over sand.
Party boats turn around across the bay, sounds of boozed
up laughter break the quiet night.

Giggles carry from boat to shore. Metallica soars from
speakers.
One gull flaps its wings between beats, the vibrations of
bone and feather
Effortless, outward bound

Around the bend, inside what is left of a bookstore, an old
man reads King Lear
Aging, decaying monarch of terrible judgment and
choices,
and others listen and imagine plots of other damaged
souls,
raped, beaten, manipulated, murdered,
some with redemption, as they listen, the eight of them,
and now me, and
Eat old popcorn and drink aged colas.

Lear wears well on this old group. The moon fits the mood. Make of it what you will.
Just a reading for some, romance for others, or
Reflections on greatness,
a fall to flattery and deceit, and a descent into madness
under a moonlit sky.

What madness surrounds the bay, in those high end condos
On the party boats, no kingdom to rule or lose
Daughters to chose, men to kill or bury

Or not?

CONSTRUCTION WORKERS

Men of hard hats calloused hands
Walk taller that collar and tie
Head forward chin down men
They move with steps of power walk with
Confidence
Whether pot bellied, dirty hand and nailed,
With Eastwood faces, lines deep and with easy smiles
It is the linearity of their days
Days where something that wasn't is
From A to B that by 5
They pick up asphalt, steel plates in place over some man
made hole, filed with wire, pipe, and circuits
A start, a finish, sweat, lunch, eyeball a few chicks on 57th,
have an afternoon beer
Then go to that other life
The tough one supported by your 25 bucks and hour
No room for anything else but the work
Straight shouldered, big sky guys
Whose weariness comes from honest effort
Not those anxieties of ambient men, with knotted guts,
Always thinking about the next thing, missing the current
one, and everything else

FOURTH FINGER LEFT HAND

Has that ring carried for 25 years through
Fishing trips, road journeys, in a car of screaming kids,
On and off planes to everywhere in search of a buck
To pay the bills, buy all the clothes and hose
And that remodeled kitchen she had to have

A slim 14k band symbol of commitment and fidelity
That was honored, while she mused about the perfect man
That never showed up, but imagined that he did
Ring in a black velvet box
But it feels still there, a phantom of a marriage gone to
hell
Like a limb blown away

The finger has its own memory, of the years, the diapers,
bills, fights, a few passionate nights
Only a few to be fair
Rubs the finger with his thumb as he drives West to some
sunset he mostly missed
Repeatedly
Wanders to a lifeguard stand coaxing a memory to return
of what life was like before the ring

Before the weight of a committed life took him away from
the other life
Now free of that
joy should be there across the cold sand
Thumb rubs fourth finger,
And tears cloud the horizon.

I WAS

Here to do grand things
When I found that was not to be
I devoted myself to other things
Small or not
That might elevate my spirit, touch the bottled soul,
And lift me towards becoming of some value

Not the stuff of epitaphs, or chiseled stone.

If the world would end
In a year and you knew it
What would you do?

Trek to Machu Picchu, see a lion in Tanzania
Track down a whore in Zanzibar or Thailand
Swim across the Bosphorus, race a Porsche at Indy?

Make up with your uncle Jake, take your grandchildren to
Disneyland,
Actually have a conversation with your exes, listen to your
children,
Give Blood, drive a meal to a senior,
feed a homeless man alone in some concrete canyon?

Get yourself to the most serene, warm place you can find,
meditate
Climb the Matterhorn and scream at the insanity of it all
Eat every damn thing you shouldn't,
drink until you cannot stand,
finally smoke a Cuban cigar,
suck on a monster bong, drop acid,
drive until you run out of gas, and forget about finding
your way home

Because there is no home, when you are running towards
oblivion.
Or all of the above?
And, of course, why wait for the end game, anyway.
It always just a deep breath away .

THE NEW DISH HITS
THE FLOOR

Loudly.

Shrimp and noodles in a lump, pieces of dark porcelain,
over two feet of kitchen floor.

Despair is everywhere.

Anger spills out of her, metaphor for your life. Everything
undone and unmentioned. Neglected issues, arguments
grown into silence, revealed. One plate of a new set
Shattered.

So is the world, by monster Muslims, killing Jews in Paris.
Je Suis Charli. The banners say.

Real hate brings good people out in the streets, to say to
the Jihadists, we will not yield to your hate and murder,
your love of blood and distortion of Allah.

Here is the faux battle of Green Bay and Dallas, this
dropped plate, broken of distraction, a mind wandering
towards some private grand destination or to a salon of
great thoughts,

always hoping that intellect is mitigation for distraction
and being anywhere but present.

Screams end. Whining commences. Apology rendered.
Silence

The teevee is an electronic bandage for domestic ills, and eyes turn to it, all else unresolved.

Pieces are picked up, the dinner wiped clean. Easier to remedy than a cluttered, over educated, distracted mind. Exigencies of cleaning, closing box tops, reheating dinner, tightening the cap on the soda, and avoiding the next calamity are a well needed reset.

Plates are replaceable,
football is a game,
Jews are still targets,
and your mind can only be one place at a time, effectively.

THAT RUT

Is about 8 " long
Stretchable to any size, from anywhere
Folded over, double, durable and thick, vein filled, warm
tunnel
That is provided by evolution to take men in, locking
them, whipping them, pulling them towards the woman
who owns it.

And all her foibles, tantrums, inequities, destroying
arguments, fade
As she knows once you are there, inside this rut, it is the
rut of all ruts.
It takes you away, to places you only know when you are
there.

An evolutionary, in and out.

A highly developed piece of anatomy that turns kings and
peasants, slaves and philosophers into the same throbbing
mess of a man
Wanting it more.
Compelled by it to put with almost any indignity to get
into it and have it
hold them tightly for a few moments of carnal goings on.

And, a few visits a month, or less, men attached so,
they will spill a lifetime of semen into it and relinquish
anything to have it.
And be in it.

THERE IS PORNO
ON THE WALLS

Off of South Street

There are photos on the walls, 20x40, 10x 12 on every
wall.
Each a scene of classic flesh, revealed, haunting faces, and
open legs, showing pubis, and mons, lips swollen, women
entered everywhere by everything from flesh to plastic .
The artist sits,
quietly, with a twinkle in his erotic eyes that spend days
creating these fantasies that are his paycheck and reality.
His wife put up with it all for decades, was his subject
in those early years, when they were both outcasts to a
puritan world.
Hefner, Bobby G, came to him. Crafted nudes unlike any
others,
Wild, hot, subjective photos, revealing the inside of our
erotic dreams.
This Tony, This Tony Ward, left his South Philly roots
and went to the places, where
he could find women of a look of abandon, decadence,
and frightening in their ferocious joy of the pursuit of his
image of sexuality.

Paris, Prague, Geneva, Moscow.

Not girls next to your door. But still he took you to them,
this artist, you became immersed, throwing yourself at
them.
Losing your fear of what it might be like with any one of
them.
Under a colossal ass in blue mesh stockings, he tells the
story.
A boy in an interracial family.
One brother schizophrenic, the other disabled.

An outlier, he was, with the gift of an erotic eye, so
unique, that found the courage, to create, all of this
From that twinkle, all of man's nerve endings are bound,
to optic nerve to brain to penis.
Universal links, but only some can see what he captures.
Some darkness we all share, an excitement we all seek, on
these walls, unmistakable.
This is good work.

OLDEST MAN

In the room . I am now.
So people think I am in charge with something to say
And then don't let me say it
Curious being gray and drawn
Energetic or not

Viewed as learned, stout and with some wealth
Often totally wrong headed
Hoping to act as if
I were an old and wise seer
A world beater

Not just the old man in the room
For show and tell.
We are multi layered, multi faceted
Sacks of molecules
A remarkable array of DNA
Driving energy through veins and organs

Eating and thinking fueling complex things
Searching for meaning
Farting, swallowing, healing a nick, twirling a hair,
scratching a butt
All at once

As cells die and divide

Blood filled with oxygen, food converted to stomach
sludge,

Air through lungs and eyes still acute enough to see a rose,
bee, and breasts passing.

Layer upon layer

Enough complexity to suggest a miracle,in each of us,
same protoplasm, after a simple life free of evil, waste, and
insignificance.

Against a billion, billion stars,

just a spec

of some sentient stardust, blown round for these years

hoping to brush up against

some purpose or relevance.

VIAGRA WOMEN

Where are they
Hiding someplace warm and faraway
The women who want men with hard ons that last for
hours
Women of the blue pills

Who talk about desire
Want their men hard and long and often
Have you bumped into one of them lately?

Ever?

Or as challenging, find a man spending 43 bucks a pill
Who is using his wood constantly coming more than once
into his favorite
Chosen vessel

Vats of blue pills, millions of doses, visions of erections,
into softly opened vaginas awaiting thrusts and sperm
hourly, and nightly

Find me just one, who wants it that way

Deliver that panting woman who wants Earl as stiff as
July corn
Where Sam can come as much as he wants into Charlene
They are out there somewhere

Viagra women, looking for wooden men
But no one can find them
If they could they would put their faces in Times Square

Save your money chumps
For a breakfast at Norm's at 2am
When you can't sleep
It will last longer
Be more satisfying
And is damn well easier to find.

NIGHT ROACHES

There is only artificial light that mocks moon glow
But the roaches don' t know their prehistoric DNA cannot
tell, so they come out,
Everywhere

Shadowing their hideous forms roaches,
this sweet quiet dog and one night walking man, who can
see them, one regular sort, contemplating Kafka,
projecting himself down there onto the halogen flooded
concrete.

Are they roaches or all of them damaged lost men
on the wrong place on that karmic wheel, transformed to
care for nothing, only to scurry to a light,
scramble for that fallen Frito Lay filet
Are they all men who were so damaged by life,unloved,
untouched, unraveling, so they beamed themselves to be
these night crawlers, under these curb holes
A twilight zone respite from the daggers of women who
never smiled, said thank you, or cared whether the
imposed solitude gave them strokes over breakfast
Did they lose, as the women went to Macy' and Kohl's,
with their life
All of them were roaches now,

once on two legs, basking in the Malibu sunlight, not
crawling.

The dog sees them and passes them by, as they scurry to a
nearby hole, by the street light.
At dawn they return to their cars, fight the freeways, work
the work. To return, each warm night
to the asphalt and tar cracks, sucking up moonlight.
Roaches, all

DOUBLE DUTCH

There is more to forget than remember
Few sweet moments, laughs from streets that scream for
order
After the gangs retreat, dealers out of bags, street walkers
wet and tired,retreat to hot showers and cloth robes

A truckload of inner city kids, find the beach for respite

So away they go towards the wind and sun lay out a towel
let the toddlers run free, chase some gulls, and mostly
laugh hard until they fill up with clean air, simple joys,
that comes
as they play Double Dutch
Weaving clothesline,that held jockey shorts
Into an afternoon of rhythm, bounce, high steps, away
from the neighborhood
Where the smiles are locked away deep inside until that
Rope turns at the beach, arcs against a blue spring sky
Another weekend day and the girls jump, the moms turn,

And some step in
They become girls again

Smile wide

And jump into a moment of pure release

And the dealers roll over in their beds, the tough guys
vomit the nights' beer, and the girls of the boulevard sleep
until 2 in the afternoon.

SALMON COLORED SKY

Over green sea
And past the red and white smokestacks
A moon rises
Full and white
Cotton candy clouds blow towards the horizon, and a chill
Overtakes us

As I try to get some romance from her
Any glance of affection
Extended arm or half face, cheek

Nothing

Comes between moon and salmon sky
Until the car turns north and we catch a breeze that sends
Perfume towards me, familiar mist
And memories pour in of closeness lost, lips parted, her
Coppertone hue from neck to knee
All in one shore breeze

The moon rises, red sky yields to dark blue night
And asleep she falls
Untouched in her bed
By any of it

SUNDAY's CANE

Orange wildflowers circle the rubber,red, oval.
Interwoven with yellow ones, above a blue sky so clear that
you get a lump in your throat and you almost cry

Two regular guys lumber, but not like me, round this
track, a rope between them.
One cannot see any of it, this day or any other.
No technicolor anything,
but then they accelerate, feet more off the ground than
on, aloft they are,friend, rope and sightless man, flying
through the laps.
I long some for that rope.
More for a buddy so reliable just for an hour or so, to
guide me, around life's oval, looking out for me at each
turn.
Such a lonely distance runner on track and life I have
become.
He pauses after two miles, and gathers his cane, and finds
his way to the car.
That blue sky lump still in my throat, what was in his or
just the clarity that comes with accomplishment.
All my belching and bitching about bumps in the road,
leaves me .

Thankful to see two men in lock step,
effortlessly, skimming over rubberized turf.
Proving to anyone in this damn universe
that you can overcome anything,
with will, a friend,
on a warm California morning.

PARROT WALKER

Why does an otherwise normal looking man
Take a parrot for a walk at the beach?
Does the parrot need a mobile perch, to sniff the ocean
air? Or see a beach girls form?

He leaps and skips from sidewalk to sand, conversing with
baby talk, turned into beak speak
No regular man is thus inclined. Does he eat, and shower
and screw with the parrot, ubiquitously?

The Long John Silver types at Venice, with the pirate
motif, I understand, it's business.
But, this is what?

Just old fashioned, eccentric bliss, one carefree dude with a
bird for a companion, alter ego, or muse?
It should be that easy for the rest of us.
Find your parrot!

LIMO LIFE

It took me 29 years to get inside a limousine, and catch a
free ride in the smaller version of the Lincoln Town car.
In Manhattan every swell had a car, the VP's and VIP's,
the junior ad execs and all the secretaries used it as a perk.
It was before cable,
CNN,
monster conglomerates, and media types on Mad Ave,
were making cash handover fist.

As the cash flowed so did the blow, the acid, high priced
dinners, the three martini lunch, paying rent for a secret
someone, and limo's.

Charlie would drive it across town or to the train, and
some nights, your boss would say, "take the car",
And we took it, to the Village, Uptown or for a ride
through the park to impress the women of the moment.
The lost ones, soulless moguls to be, used the back seat for
all positions, rubbing of skins, and release of fluids.
Mostly, I took it to the late train, talked up politics and
Ed Koch, heard Charlie out on what was really wrong
with the city, and felt like a shooter, drinking bubbled
water in a glass.
Now when I get in a limo, rarely, it is all flashback,

the smell of leather, that deep breath that comes from being off a Manhattan street,

gazing at the Trump Tower up Fifth, that reverie of party time,

High times.

When you thought you were somebody, owned a piece of that ebb and flow,

Because you had a driver, named Charlie, and the car for the night.

STARTLED

After 21 years, at 2am I am staring at the ceiling
planning, stalking some future project
Then she jumps and screams possessed by some storyline
into a night horror film plying in her head

This time I am actually there, to hold her, and put my lips
on her cheek
For one frozen frame we are those two kids in love again,
in her blue bed overlooking 3rd avenue,
Lost in that embrace of surety, that shuts off the kids,
deaths, and inane sentences of marriage dialogue that
become your conversation

Then she rolls away, and starts to snore

And I am back alone with that ceiling and eventually, my
dreams

JOEY

No one believes this, certainly not my teens, with their X
box games, pierced brows, and scooters.
Everything now a cartoon, packaged and shrink wrapped,
Playboy, Twinkies and even pickles., without barrels.
It is a processed world, nothing is loose, everything
packaged and marketed
no tie between product and producer.
Everything from some, one factory in Taiwan or Korea.

So when I say there was a horse that pulled a milk wagon,
up a halfway finished Philly street, they moan.

All head and hoof
Big teeth and cold, wet nose
My first main attraction, and I saved an apple each week
to feed to him
And every Friday for a few ..years.. he would eat it out of
hand
Right there in the street, from my hand to his big teeth,

And a hug,

and then a handshake from Johnny, the milkman with an
iron right hand, blown off at Guadalcanal

It was linear then, a horse, a kid, an apple, a vet, a bottle
of milk

The straight lines are gone now

XMAS IN PALM SPRINGS

You can find desert here past the spas and thick towels
Outside casinos ringing in a payday, for once beaten tribes,
Away from tanned, busty, bejeweled wives, across the
highway from artificially watered greens and golfers in
high fashion, multi- colored pants

There is a desert.
I'm in it running over sand tracks to a far tree line, from
telephone pole to scrub pine, with a Trump 29 sign as my
North Star.
Serenity enters when attached to nothing. Thoughts come
and go, there is nothingness here, easily accessed.
Each stride offers a release from obligations of another
year of support, earning, trying to hold on after 55 to
something that suggests a future
Warrior motif,running almost bare in December,
dropping clothes along the way, yields to the complicated,
exasperated, homo modern,
stuck still in a present, far too familiar and known,
longing to go far back to the native spirit, and harness it to
inform the next steps into tomorrow.
The sun and the dust envelop these old bones and offer,
if no answers, enough warmth to end this year and begin
again.

LIGHTNESS

Walk down 5th avenue for a few years, and you see
Everyone carries a weight on their backs
Atlas like they push on with long faces and world weary
stares
By Rockefeller Center the statue stands, but his face you
see is not pained

The Gods gave Atlas the world, and that was that, not as
burden but duty

For mortals we carry whatever burdens we want, name it,
someone carries it. Some put the burden there to define
them. It offers purpose
No God gave it to them, they invented it, defined it
Who wants that or them?
You can carry life's woes as a pile of bricks, build a fort
with them or even build a wall with them, and then
decide if you are screaming
to get out or afraid to let anyone else into your life .
Keep your self imposed burdens, your walls within walls,
your self imposed, self importance.

Look to the others who are light hearted and hardy
Whatever life brings them, death, cancer, loss, poverty,
they rebound
Whether imprisoned wrongly, surviving the Hanoi
Hilton, or just caught in the struggle to make ends meet,
they can find some light. They bear their burden, it suits
them.

Replace Atlas with them

People with necks that will not bend, spirits that refuse to
be extinguished, it is not the world's weight they bear, but
their own, with a stunning, heroic resilience
The great success comes not by becoming Atlas, and
bearing the Gods burden, but having your own and lift it
with the power within you that is fueled by the lightness
of your being.

HEY CHAMP

Celebrities up close can evaporate your perception of them
Some are harsh and distant, others, most self conscious
and shy
But champs who are boxers do not disappoint

At Caesar's Larry Holmes came at me, winding through
the crap tables. It was all hugs and handshake,
As though we knew each other. Then, he drifted into a sea
of gamblers from Japan, and they screamed at him,like a
rock star

At the Verrazano Bridge, in the rain, awaiting the start
of the NYC marathon, a heavy, thick, man stood in the
drizzle, on his sweatshirt it said simply, "Champ"
There was broad smile, and Swedish accent, and an
enormous right hand reached mine, Ingemar Johansson it
was. And I told him how I watched him take out Floyd,
watching a black and white television on a neighbor's
stoop.
Humble, and sweet, he nibbled at a jelly donut as his
preparation for his marathon run, and talked me through
that championship round, blow by blow. I was carried for
ten miles on that encounter

Then it is 6:40 am in Las Vegas, I am out the door for a jog, a limo pulls in
Two men exit, look right and left. I pause. Time stops.
Ali gets out of the car, walks a few steps. I run to him.
The body guards grab my arms.
Ali motions towards me, I shake his hand, and can only utter, "I love you Champ"
He puts my head in a faux headlock and lets me go, laughing.
Then says, " go get in that road work, before you get too old to run"
And I head off down the strip, striking at the wind, pretending to be working a boxer's run not mine.

And then,
One summer it is 110, under a tent behind Caesar's. two dozen children from a Boy's Club get out of a bus and run to the practice ring. No one is there. Until
An old man is wheeled into the place, and behind two men with an ice cream cart. Treat enough, I suppose.
Then the ice cream man, introduces the man in the wheelchair. There is a silence, the heat rises.
"This is Joe Louis . The greatest fighter of all time."
They line up and he gives each child a cone and a kiss on the forehead.

This once Brown Bomber, serving ice cream in the
Vegas heat. I wait until, they are served and cautiously
approach him.
I thank him for all those years, and he nods.
I say no to some ice cream.

In chair or not, it was unmistakable, that this one man
was still giving, offering, whether cone or memories to all
around
If you can transmit greatness through a closed fist, a nod,
a hug or even a smile; their greatest power was never,
ever just in the ring.
How many, so called icons today, can offer or match any
of that?

THE INCONSEQUENTIAL LIFE

Atop the podium is a thick wasted, fat faced, balding,
millionaire
So help me God
I am watching him wondering, why him, not me.
This life of mine without much consequence, wasted in
most ways, intellect, power of speech and word, demeanor,
a look of someone bold, a familiar, symmetrical face, lean
enough,
Applied to what of lasting merit ?

Applied to nothing of substance, without legacy,
ephemeral, or

Designed to lead and challenge, oratory and presence lost
to luncheons and meetings, endless
In the stars was there not something grander,
brought by a celestial force,
kingly traits dissipated by fear of becoming something in
the foreground and into the spotlight

Stunted by small choices, untapped abilities, fear wins,
shame enslaves
There was never an epiphany, no woman behind the man,
no Manchurian candidature to be had
A self view stymied by self doubt, and a conditioned mind

Obsession comes with the DNA or not, needed to rocket
to altitude and fly into grand plans, greatness, and a
metric on life, of value
No constitutional oath left only
I swear to wake up and make it through another day
So help me God

COUNTRY IS A
STATE OF MIND

On Wall Street they wear cowboy boots
In Denver gals wear ten gallon hats
Down in Phoenix, Texas ties are still vogue
Over in LA, well, they wear it all

Some say there is no country anymore
The west of Wild Bill and Oakley are long gone
Replaced by
Skyscrapers, dealmakers, white collars, and cars from
overseas

To all of that I say

Country is a state of mind

If you believe it and want
It is always there
Somewhere

Country is a state of mind
Where that ole flag still is revered
Where God lives within
And love and family and freedom still rule

Wherever you go,
loving friend or fighting foes
From Odessa to Kabul, Fort Smith to Boise, Idaho
Country is a state of mind

No one takes that train to Abilene
Laughs at Gabby Hayes or Minnie Pearl
Or boozes hardy like Hank did
Anymore
Still I know, there is country out there in millions of
hearts
Wherever, they may be,
Country is just a state of mind

THERE ARE MORE OF US

Who never get

Laid enough

Paid enough

Cry enough

Yell enough

Drink enough

Fill in your

Enough

Go ahead

Put in your own not enough of

Express, decompress, unload, kickback,

Just

Relax

Enough

There are some I am certain

Who get enough of everything, but probably do not

understand enough or

Appreciate enough or

Care enough

About the rest of us

Enough already,

Enough

BAKER

Red lights point towards Vegas
Mojave darkness strobes on a line of ten thousand cars,
back up lights
A semi blocks everything just west of Jane, even the
Highway radio 89.9
Can't jump start me, weary from an LA week. Past that
thermometer, over across the street from Big Boy,

Christina has my key, to a Hitchcock hotel, a few RV's, an
old Chevy as neighbors for the night
Dry beer smell penetrates the room in my number 16
The shower works, the floor is clean,
I fit here, no Motel 6, no light on for ya

By 2 am, the bed seems inviting the old movies on GRIT
TV, even to corny for me
Loading the .38, content with these companions, Mr.
Smith and Mr. Wesson,
Pretending, this is the Sierra Madre, and I'm Bogart about
to get to ACT III

Only that black crow knows, out the window, how many
fantasies these rooms have seen, or more likely were
dreamed, in the minds of all those road worn men
Waiting for the semi to be moved, the red lights to fade,
and the sun to rise over Baker

THE MONKS

Cut you up, in big chunks, biceps, thighs, and butt
One gutted torso, headless, on a hammock high, in the
cold, under white thin clouds
The scavengers come and pick at your parts as you transit
on the Karmic wheel to that next life
Without much ceremony, no matter who you are or were,
you are now bird food, protein.

The Monks know the shell, the mortal coil is worthless,
the soul or its counterpart gone with death
No need to preserve any of it, bury it, waste wood, land,
or any resource
They like the Vikings knew the corpus worthless, Kirk
Douglas in a long boat, as Tony Curtis sends flaming
arrows, setting the vessel ablaze, and the dog barks as his
master burns

And down a street in a humid city, past marble
monuments to the dead, a wagon rolls, one black horse,
with boots backwards, precede the casket of one well liked
decent man, so a nation can mourn his passing.
What civilized men do, perhaps too much
Remember who he was, helped, saved, touched, warred
against, stood for, loved and changed

So we would not let go of him without ceremony,
he was shipped here UPS style
We would have remembered him as much, cried the
same tears, if we chopped up our fallen, and built no
monuments, cut no stone, blasted no mountain to deify
them
What if he had been chopped up for the birds, atop some
Western peak, as the sun set, letting his spirit soar
Run through the souls of the men who rule in his place.
Would he be less remembered or more ?
All that can be preserved, studied, and revered is
merely memory,
and the essence of a life well lived
that becomes part of us.

OH YEAH THAT'S
THE GOVERNOR

Over there, 15 feet away
In shorts on that bike, tan, smiling,
Comfortable really with his children and their friends,
surrounded by bikers, surfers, strollers, still, he seems
untouched by it, so used to celebrity, he is

No one says hello, runs towards him, or creates a scene
Even in West LA, this 20 million a picture man would
ring a crowd, but not today
He is the Governor, not that other guy and right now
A father, just a father, out for a bike ride on the Strand
with is kids

Even that long black GMC, and the guys riding behind
him, do not take away this simple day at the beach
No casino bills, workman comps debates, legislative woes
or the No's of running the state
Not today
Leave him alone

So he can pretend, suspend reality, in this life of his, and

concentrate on nothing more than that kiss, he just got

from his youngest on his cheek, and the universal

"I love you daddy"

And let his face soften, as he waves to no one but his sons

SO I AM OUT OF SHIRTS

Again.

15 light starched, whites, solids, and few pinstripes. And one with a white collar, over a field of blue.

Too damn lazy to pick them off the floor, distracted enough to not pick up the ones locked in the dry cleaners store

Without them, corporate poses, dissolve, tie culture abates, and black T-shirt replaces pomp, jeans force another mood

You can dream about luscious women, white beaches is a cliché.

What would it be like to never have another dry cleaning ticket, no more starched and pressed life, leaving the 15 shirts and ten more forever?

Letting Kiki, at Jose's laundry, wonder why I never returned and that some South Sea Island finally became my Bali Hai.

VELVET ROPES

There are lines to cross in sand, drawn in anger fueled by
bravado,
Some afraid to cross or be crossed. Imaginary markers
setting limits, as long and high as any wall, created by
others to
Box us in or keep us out. Lines of rejection, subjection,
holding back punches, jabs and even kisses
Real ones put there by owners, social climbers, intent
upon choosing who passes to dine, dance and smoke

Velvet with brass, denying a pass to the select few, who
look, breasts and lips, or have enough juice of some sort to
fit in
Every line is a garret tossed on a neck, pulled tight to
control
Tear down the line, velvet or rope, yellow police tape, or
finger drawn demarcation line in the sand.
Knock them down.. cross

JUST NORTH OF VALHALLA

There is a left turn where souls gather off the parkway
All wet stones, soaked, by another spring rain
Everything colored charcoal, sky, trees, lawn,
Blue eyes turned black, a 19 year old smile and essence,
consumed by time and dirt
Still I come knowing there is really nothing here, but,
myth that something lingers that is knowable
In places like this

What I know is that tears will come, no sobs suppressed,
burning eye and cheek as they fall
The old tree over him is uprooted, and one, younger, full
of the thorns of spring remains,
Running my hand across them, to feel if I am really there
For ritual I pull, a few stones from a mountain we climbed
together
Tap the grave with one to announce our presence,
medieval rite…
to another, as I read the Hebrew death prayer, Kaddish,
connecting both of us to all the others dead from
Abraham to him

Nothing helps, really
Not the tears, the damnations I utter into the wet wind,
not the hard rain

Everything is grey, wet and cold, North of Valhalla
So I leave him to the wind, the rattle of the trains bound
for Manhattan
One father, alone, with his son

ONE ARMED STREETWALKER, WHERE ARE YOU, GIRL?

Who strolled in half steps at 58th and Central Park

After all these years, watching her go through the seasons,
in a Black Gama fur, always a thin silk summer dress
without stockings, in 4 " come get me heels
Always blonde, alabaster skin, like marble her complexion,
enough breast to attract, and a shawl that hid her short
arm until the John was hooked
It never seemed odd or perverse, what does a woman of
the night need with two hands, anyway
Most men want holes,
one hand will do

On this NYC street nothing stays the same, not the
restaurant she walked by, not the bodega that was once
owned by a Korean, then Vietnamese, now Persian.
Not the old hotel, now Trump something or another,#8

It was foolish to think, she would still be here either, now that I am old enough to make an offer, old enough to need a gentle touch, even from, a veteran of this street without an arm, who survived for years,

now

The only emotional amputee left on this corner is me.

THE LOCKER RULE

There are 22 lockers this Sunday afternoon
empty
You pick one, so you can go hit the heavy bag, to knock
away another week, the movement, the smacks bring back
some balance and restore the circuits that have not fired
for a while
Action, reaction, physics, motion, and the sweat comes
With it a cleansing, the edges are smoothed

Shower ready, that locker now has a lock next to it
Not two away, next to it
Is there some rule, that someone always will
Pick the locker next to yours

That no matter what you do, to force yourself somewhere
else the choice you make
Always seems to bump against a guy who just must be
next to you
A guy dripping from his swim, wide as a bowling alley
Excusing himself into your space

The forces return, with but another indignity, small
though it is
And there is just no escape

NOBODY SLEEPS TONIGHT

Nessun Dorma
        Rossini was pissed
                A frog sang a high note in Guillaume Tell

Louis Duprez was the first with a sound of his chest voice
High C

He had his balls intact offering a man's sound
Only a few had that note within them
Corelli, Kraus, Bjoerling

Notice there is no Caruso who struggled mightly to reach
the classic
High "do"

Then one tenor emerged of enormous chest and tone
Designed he was by providence to be champion of the
note
Pour mon ame' requires 9 in a row to be achieved as
Donizetti wrote them

Luciano belted them to an audience at the Met,
overwhelmed by his gifts

Of head, chest, and voice, no one else now or since could conquer this tonal
Everest,
Yet, he did, for decades
You could not sleep nor want to when he sang, anything, even in his death, his notes reverberate through the ages.

EACH RUN

Should be run as though it is the last

Each step the here and now

Every breath the final in and out

Not on the way to anywhere, or anything, not preparing

for future races, or training with purpose

Run as though it is the last

Expectation gone

Time stopped

Distance unnoticed

Each run as though it is the last

Free of training regime

Effort and desire to improve

Eliminating hubris, and expectation

Steps to savor, quietly, elongated strides

Unrushed, steps

Mind clearing, towards only some

Exhilaration, leading to a trip through and across time

One breath, one step,

Going nowhere

Mushu, nothingness

Release, nirvana

Pure

THE ROCK STREWN PATH

Is all boulder, pebble, over dust, covering dirt and inland
sand
Not a smooth foot fall anywhere as it snakes towards some
rotted Jeeps at a place where actors played MASH, war
surgeons, where mountains by an American sea stood in
for Korea
You can run this path,
like any other, pretend it is smooth and straight. Fool
striding ahead to a simple goal, where trail stops and turns
upward to a cobalt sky
Then trips on stone and smashes soft, face and brow, cut
bloody by nature's right hook
You can run this rock strewn path, like some fool, willing
it smooth when it is not, forcing you to a bloody result.
All damage of your making, blood in your mouth,
copious, bright red
Adapting does not make you weaker or
Avoiding the obvious stronger, just sore, with a bruised face,
A boxers cut, on a face you have seen all these years, force
together the gash,
Now scared again by taking on the forces and
Losing
The path is either smooth or not
And wishing will not make it so

XMAS BY THE SEA

The ocean rises in eight foot swells
Blue/green white foam capped walls carry men of varying
size on fiberglass boards
They descend at high speed, breaking right
tossed at rides end and back into the sea.

Thin women await them around a fire pit, all goosebumps
and hard nipples through those bikini bottoms that do
not seem out of place here, even in December

Other little girls, ride a Xmas bike, all pink with training
wheels- guiding her way along the strand
Streamers, purple, green and white, stiffen from handlebar
and fender. Mom, Dad, jog along side, forgetting this will
be some grand memory, when their daughters have grown
to fill wetsuits and bikini, sit by their fire sand watch the
surf rise

At volleyball nets everyone seems to have a Santa hat,
proclaiming the observance,along this six miles of beach.
Yet, only two women play in thong and bra, attracting
welcome stares of men on bikes or foot, their Santa hats as
red as their ample butts

The homeless guy with the white beard unwraps a
lunch of old pizza, coated in sand, garlic bread and a
lone orange. This is his usual spot, along this stretch of
Manhattan Beach, if he knows it is Xmas you cannot tell
A bulldog with a jingle bell collar decides to crap by the
old guys bike.
His owner takes out a a zip lock bag and scoops it up,
curses, perhaps reflecting in the Xmas ham he fed the
animal, or his girlfriend, Joy, who fed him chocolate

A wind blows sand over the crap that remains, the old
man dusts off his slice, those little girls catch their Dad,
giggling all the way. A classic looking surfer dude take
off his wetsuit at the shower, smiles at everyone, warmly,
the salt yields to the water, and on his back the globe and
anchor of a Marine.
There is not a scream, a bark, or a tear anywhere.
Merry Xmas

TRIUMPH

We all want to triumph over something
Mostly our own fears, our own nature, to evolve to a
higher plane be elevated, elongated, escalated
Real triumphs in that realm, but, we substitute, always
substituting and sublimating one fear for another one flaw
for a tangential challenge
I do not want to climb Everest like Hilary and Norgay
Hit 714 like Ruth and Aaron
Swim for 8 medals like Spitz or even save the free world
Like Churchill and FDR
Find that unified theory, or erase cancer with a fully
engineered genome
One simple triumph by me over me to stop being
Afraid of failing, falling, into a meaningless life, and find
some glorious hope, not up a mountain
Or swimming to Cuba, but in my mirror
That getting up is for something, anything besides the
economic to and fro
Not a consumptive nothing
Instead towards some psychic peak, of my making
That satisfies and completes, owned, wanted and desired
Triumph of existence, when the whining stops, and
responsibility is taken

CIGARS AND TURPENTINE

No sea breeze, flags limp above life guard stands, everyone
gone to sell ideas, screenplays, wait tables, turn California
on, keep their mortgages
Women in black dresses, swimsuits on the bedroom
floors,
Boards on porches, sandy trucks and wet T- shirts in a
pile, now replaced by Khakis, socks, and GAP blazers
All off in leased cars, leaving behind the crap of a
weekend, men in faded jeans, some with work belts,
calloused hands, building more fashionable places by the
sea, their hats turned backwards, these men of easy smiles,
with cigars in their lips or between fingers
An aroma of hard work, the simple grace of hammering a
nail with one stroke into a 4x8
Cigars mixed with turpentine odors and that pleasant
sawdust smell from sawed wood, that penetrates the few
nostrils that come past on a Wednesday at ten am.
These working men, many whiffs and puffs away from
the cappuccino's ; the garlic loafs; and steaks grilled at the
posh places

Here are linear days of straight edges, nails, some glue,
and turpentine, the accomplished day of the average Joe
and Jose'
And the cigars smell heavenly as the offshore flow picks
up at Sunset and blows it all out to sea
The flags pick up wind and the 405 is jammed.

ONE GREAT OLD MONK

It is still a cold, grey place where Tzars and Cossacks
pushed peasants and Jews around
A land of pogroms, sabers, and Potemkin villages, with
winters long
Over harsh, expansive plains

Stopping every megalomaniac, Napolean and Hitler
Alike

After Glassnost, there are more cigarettes, grey meat, and
leggy whores
But that chest pounding angst remains, creasing faces of
even the young
So there is this clear fermented stuff
180 proof, Russian water
Vodka

That in 1503 stopped being an antiseptic and became this
on the rocks
An elixir, passing the Tzars lips, and revolutionary,
anarchist alike
Drink to that lone monk who in a Russian Fall,
contemplating the winter ahead
Began pouring it into glasses and jars

For Lenin, Trotsky, Bukharin, Nikita, even
Rachmaninoff, Shostakovich, Yeltsin, who had too much
of it
And
Putin
From potato fields of the common man a drink for men
and royalty,
Proletariat, and bourgeoisie
Das Vedanya

OLD ROSES

Thick, tough stalks once tender and lean, once pliable
protective points
Now 30 years in California soil, still protecting its rose
Each stalk rising, reaching for sun and life again and
again
An explosion of petal and color, scented
Even cut back each winter, sawed off to stumps, somehow
rising, without effort or notice to return
Nature worries not that they will return, inexorably
Watching every cycle in an old canvas chair by them, as
the mortgage is payed, the children raised,
No fear they will not, only if I will return, recycle and
grow, where are my thorns

I have my gnarled,sturdy stalks, but how many buds, can
this aging bush bring
Some more, even one this spring
One more, one more, white rose.

IT'S LINEAR, MAN

When you are young everything is one straight line
Linear man
Your hormones kick up,
you see Thea's ass,
or want to see Elaine's nipples, you pursue in car and at
the movie house, and even in your buddy' s basement lair,
and you get there

Linear

You rush through school, avoid studying anything except
how to avoid studying, get out, make a buck and catch the
career train

Linear

And you are just smart enough and lucky as well to get on
the train to some cash, a few fast multiple lays, a few rare
blow jobs; some VP stripes; a loving wife or two and some
excellent kids, the whole grey flannel suit trip
Linear

So you are at point M from A on your way to N. But the
way to N is a sharp right to Nowhereland

With an arrow pointing South
Everything that was up the dialectic to the right is an
effort now. That famous dick is largely unused, your jobs
fewer, the kids find you useless, money is draining.

No money, no life

No stripes no perks
Scary unholy mess
Stocastic now, jagged and crooked, what happened to
Linear?

Hobbling from one place in life to another,one idea zig
zagging to another
The freedom of the open path frightens, but it could be
better, really

Meandering

Sideways can work, go left for income, right for joy, throw
away the old ways
Just stop man
Drawing a life line from A to Z. that's the trapped way.
Give it up- zig- when the world zags

Run up across and down. Sleep through some of it
Mostly stop moaning

Crying, whining,
For N O P Q R S T......
It's gone man
Lost linear and
Its never coming back
Zig

ONE NIGHT IN HARRISBURG

There were five of us, all 18 years old or so, in this one
room, on two beds, smelled of moths balls
Off to Vietnam, we were headed. OCS for me,

if I passed the physical.

Nervous talk of girls, and bravado, the talk before a
football game or backyard fist fight
All eyes open.

Even the 250 pounder, sat with his hands behind his head,
the streetlights on his face
The local kid threw up a night of beer, until the dry
heaves kicked in
Endless night, until a starched regular Army guy yelled
from a van to come down at dawn

A Catch 22 scene at the induction center, boys trying to
be brave and manlike in jockey shorts.
Passed all the checkpoints, until a surgeon examined my
left arm
"what is this son"
"an old injury, sir, broken forearm"

The Sargent thought it was a ruse, so he sent me in a truck
for a 50 minute ride to a hospital X-ray room

Others were given a bag with three postcards and three
stamps. They were told to write one home now and one
when they get on base.
Off they were to Da Nang

Back at State College, the recruiter called and had me
come to see him, where with sadness, he said I was
declared 4-F, no pronate motion of the arm, made me
unfit.
What happened on a ball field few years ago, a dumb fight
between me and a bat, kept me from Vietnam, and some
fate unknown of valor, death, or PTSD
I did not feel lucky
I kept it all a secret from everyone, all of it
Until, I read about that fellow who dry heaved all night,
turned up dead in the Tet offensive
When I smell stale beer, or mothballs, I think of him
The nervous sweat of that one night
And the war I missed,over a few broken bones

235

AND THE IMPORTANT THINGS SEEM

To happen at the wrong time
Forced to read Homer and Joyce, Euripides, and Chaucer,
Pound, and Longfellow
Their words lost in a flood of hormones and inattention
Carrying garbage pails, trash and mowing lawns, a simple
life, where one physical exertion was followed by a payday

Regular checks, regular, sex, metered life,
lost to some ambition, with hubris and avarice and the
acquisition of:
Homes, children, awards, cars, avoiding everything,
missing life lessons, obvious and pure
Each kindness, every sorrow, all bone weary lows and
cloudless skies, a moment off, time shifted away retarding
growth, feeling, being, even
Able to grasp what matters, is not nothing, there is no
void, only the inability to

STOP

The vibrations, the bouncing ball, rattling pans, keeping
me from getting it all the time.

DREAM BLENDER

Where do the dreams go
Collected over years
Big ass ideas of contribution
Serenity focused, and full of bliss
Mashed, smashed
By life lived
Straight and narrow lined

Turned by loves
Deaths, moments of crossroad choices
Gone wrong or right
Married or not
Babies strolled, sent upright and grown along their
pathway

When stalled, destroyed, wandering, wondering still
Aimless is it?

Throw it all into life's blender
Liquefy it, smoothly mixed
Particles of dull grey, rainbow chunks of decisions
Over salted, too sweet or sour
A distasteful brew

One part ambition
Two parts devotion
Three parts ability

All overtaken by a grand mixer of influences and forces
Whipping everything into a brew served cold
All bottled up
Consumed in a gulp
And returned into toilet bowl
Down into a gutter where all that is missed and broken
flows
Into the rivers that flow to hell.

PICASSO HAD A FATHER

April 1965

Pablo paints the face of man. It is his father.

And every face after, is his father in some regard.

He is known for women, passionately rendered who he screwed

And for scribbles of all sorts

Sculpture of goats and outrage the size of a wall

Guernica

But it is always Jose' Ruiz y Blasco's eyes in his portraits of men

This father who gave Pablo his first lesson in sketching at age 7

Blasco painted birds, doves mostly, obsessed with them

Could he know what genes he had passed along

And what Picasso would do with them?

Even genius cannot deny the father, no matter how he tried

At the end of each brush stroke, Jose' appeared, whether he wanted him

On that canvas or not.

DOGMA

There is no calm quiet place where there is coffee
Always some loud mouth named Vern or Hal
Nursing a grande something and spouting some of his
DOGMA

About Christ, The Trinity, Canadian health care or his
surefire stock on the Frankfurt Exchange

DOGMA

Is about that balloon of ego filling his thoughts with so
much hot air to prove to whomever is in range how big
and expansive the howler is
The more he expounds, the closer he comes to exploding,
his views and his self image
Yet is just air, spewed into a wind that will carry away the
thoughts, ill formed, out to that vast sea of other dogmas
lost, in their stupidity to a sea of uninformed ideas

Of no merit, except the support of a malformed
personality, only a spilled cup can shut him up,
Certainly worth the effort.

HARI KARI

Sepaku,
Kneel on a mat, pull out the short sword, stab at the right
above the hepatic fissure, turn the blade slowly, pull it up,
with a sawing motion to the left
The blood will be very warm and red
Then some weaker men fall over and bleed to death,
The studied, humiliated man, pulls out his guts, all of it
and stays erect, says his final prayers and then
Dies

Never understood it, this part of Bushido, this need to end
life with a ritual rather
than just go

now I do, taboos gone, as precious as it is, once you have
so screwed up

so fucked up, there is a nobility in it

your insignificance is acknowledged, and your sullen, dark
presence, releasing everyone to a better day without you

the Japanese have this one right, making it very tough
to leave, without pain and courage to endure your own
demise, by your own knife
there are no short, sharp swords here, even the butter
knives are dull,
fortunate, huh

FOR A REASON

To all the cosmologists, pastors, well meaning assholes
who give eulogies at their friends funerals
Who always say to the assembled
"everything happens for a reason"\contemplate this

38 year old man, Jeff Miller, whose mom treated him
poorly and beat him with a bat,
Decided to rob a home, sneak in through a window, rifle a
few drawers, found some silverware
Then came upon the 82 year old widow there, the
daughter of a family all murdered by the Nazi's in
Czechoslovakia, into her cottage in Southern California,
he broke in
she felt safe that July afternoon,
No worries
Then, Jeffery shattered her world, as he threw her to the
floor, beat her, broke her ribs
He did not leave,
he put on her yellow gardening gloves, pulled off her
clothes and penetrated her
Repeatedly

She did not scream, or whimper, bravely she waited
for him to stop, the voices inside his tormented head
eventually went quiet
She survived because she could
He gets 62 years
And the purpose of this was what rabbi?
The reason was, pastor?
So we would know the horror men can do
Did she or we need that lesson again
Or would she have been just fine getting to 83, watching
her soap operas, tending her garden in her favorite yellow
gloves
And this was just not meant to be, this one time

THERE IS NOTHING

You cannot do
Or overcome
Usually on most days
It takes desire and some grit to stay with whatever the hell
it is you want to get done
You have to be maniacal in your faith to overcome any
obstacle
Not fear idealism and the passion required to persevere
Be contrarian

Unconventional and have confidence

But know that it requires work, and lots of it
Confidence as well, and rebellion, luck will find you
Be direct and unmoved by the critics and those who want
you to fail
Because if you ever succeed they will be less

And that they cannot stand

Stand for yourself, it is your dream, no one else cares,
except you
Reject the mainstream, the worn paths,
Find one with heart and go after it as if
You will die if you do not

THE FOUR HORSEMEN

You know them, the horsemen of literature, the bible, and video games
Revelation describes them on horses white, red, black, and pale
War, famine, death, for certain
And Conquest, still open to debate among scholars

Not likely to come for us, unless Jesus is returning sooner than later

What we face is daunting, and these raiders come to cut our souls to pieces

Greed, Shame, Fear, and Ostracism

You know them applied by those who want to crush the spirit
She appeals to what we want, and how much more of it we can have
The catch
It only comes through her

Shame enters as a boy and never leaves

All what we might try or do, and when we venture and fail

She comes to strip us naked, laugh at our bodies and celebrate embarrassment

Fear is ubiquitous, that rides into our lives shoulder to shoulder with shame

Haunting us, discouraging actions, what we learn, try, experience, love or not,

Boxing in what we create, impregnate, advocate, ameliorate

And if we fight it all, we are cut out, stranded from her world, which is the world we want to roam

Defying the horsemen, failing compliance, ostracism send us to life on an ice flow, in an existential sea of uncertainty, unfulfilled desire, and eventually

Madness

Until revelation, and the seals are broken

Be fearless,

or become a pawn in a life planned by someone for you

That will require Christ to save you from yourself

THE UN GANG

Before I was 15, I would take walks down a long
Boulevard named for FDR
It divided the Jews,mostly, from Oxford Circle with the
Roman Catholics from Father Judge
This was a danger zone as small gangs of thugs roamed
To rob, but, mostly just to terrorize
They were defined by places or corners
Horn and Hardart, H and H
Kensington and Allegheny, K and A

And the gang of a guy named Reds, who wore his Father
Judge jacket and liked to kick Jews in the head
And adopted the name UN for his bastards
They would send out a grade school kid to set you up,
Often have an egg in his hand, and crush it and blame
you, and scream

then they would round the corner and swarm you, until
you curled up in a protective ball, and took a few kicks
from Reds.
We all tired of the beatings, enlisted older brothers and
our own gangs, or clubs
And retaliated

In a year or so, we were strong enough, lifted weights, learned American Combat Judo, went after them, beat the ones you remembered until there was blood on the concrete

Reds had his ear bitten off in a rumble, and died when I was in college of cancer. Some of the guys who never left the neighborhood, actually pissed on his grave. It didn't seem like hate, or even particularly, wrong, any of it, then. Just boys, becoming men, the hard way.

I AM NOT A TARTIGRADES

As small as a speck of sand
Able to survive eons
Climates tropical and ice age
Can hibernate in a dormant state

Without effort they enter
Anhydrobiosos
Suspended they are, unconscious we suppose
But ultimate survivors, as grotesque they are
All portals and orifice,like a microscopic Jabba the Hut

Take me off the karmic wheel
Better bird or even roach become
Than this tardigrade who lives and thrives
With little to survive, and nothing else to do but
Be.

DISPATCH: SITTING BULL IS KILLED

In a building on the Res, or what they forced him to
Tantaka Iyotake, Hunkpapa Lakota, still had visions of a
better time

Refused to surrender took his people here to this forsaken
place
After Custer, touring with Wild Bill, and being a bona
fide Western icon and celebrity

But the establishment could not allow that he might join
Wovoka, and his Ghost Dance movement
They wanted to return to the past, unify spirits gone and
living, and purge the plains of the white man
The authorities afraid they were, worried they were of this
hoopla and Native American voodoo
Mostly afraid of Sitting Bull still

39 cops and four volunteers came for him
Shot him in the head and chest
Warriors return fire, kill 9 of them and the one who takes
Tantaka Iyotake, dies as well

So afraid they were of this aging warrior

Frightened by a dance of braves

Fooling themselves that a bullet or two would change
what they had done

No bullet killed his spirit, memory outlived the wounds

Ghost dance faded, as did the noble tribes, the victims of
a destiny

Their Gods would not let them have, other than to fade
away, surrender or stand tall

Like Sitting Bull and take a final bullet .

WHY POETRY?

The times are tough
Always are for regular folks
People of color, immigrants,
Soldiers, Marines, mothers,

Everybody on a wage, all part timers,
All without a thin dimers, moonlighters,
All sales people, and the homeless
We are over taxed, under represented,
Afraid of what's next or how to pay for it
Pray for health, a good warm meal, and
A hug, or some gesture that might reveal we matter
To anyone but just ourselves

And the world is out of sync
Old alliances make no sense
Whoever balanced the powers has lost the code
Wars from Kabul to Gaza
Radical Islam undaunted, Bin Laden ' s son now leads
them
Endless torture, sorrow, as regimes that should die do not

And who has time for poetry or any approximation of it
To write or read, worthy or not

As much time or more for the lousy as the well done
Ancient craft, words spilled and sputtered through the
worst of it
Pogrom to purge, darkness and age, pestilence and
penicillin
Holocaust and Internet

That a word, a phrase, might lighten,
Compel or offer,
solace is all
Nothing more, just that
Sorting out the present
Expecting another day
Enough

Printed in the United States
By Bookmasters